TECHNOLOGY AND TERRORISM

TECHNOLOGY
AND
TERRORISM

Edited by
PAUL WILKINSON

FRANK CASS

First published 1993 in Great Britain by
FRANK CASS & CO. LTD
Gainsborough House, 11 Gainsborough Road,
London E11 1RS, England

and in the United States of America by
FRANK CASS
c/o International Specialized Book Services, Inc.,
5804 N.E. Hassalo Street,
Portland, Oregon 97213–3644

British Library Cataloguing in Publication Data

Technology and Terrorism. – (Terrorism &
Political Violence Series, ISSN 0954-6553;
No.5)
I. Wilkinson, Paul II. Series
322.4

ISBN 0-7146-4552-4

Library of Congress Cataloging-in-Publication Data

Technology and terrorism / edited by Paul Wilkinson.
    p.   cm.
Includes bibliographical references and index.
ISBN 0-7146-4552-4 : $35.00
1. Terrorism — Prevention.   2. Terrorism — Technological
innovations.   3. Terrorism — Security measures.   4. Weapons.
HV6431.T433   1993
363.3'2 — dc20
                                                        93-28481
                                                        CIP

This group of studies first appeared in a Special Issue on 'Technology and Terrorism' of *Terrorism and Political Violence*, Vol.5, No.2 (Summer 1993), published by Frank Cass & Co. Ltd.

Typeset by SX Composing Ltd, Rayleigh, Essex
Printed in Great Britain by
Antony Rowe Ltd, Chippenham

CONTENTS

Acknowledgements

It is a sad comment that the publication of a volume of this kind would have been appropriate at any time in the past 25 years. However, in view of the fact that while this work was being prepared for the press the world experienced during spring 1993 the World Trade Center bombing in New York, a second massive IRA bomb in the City of London's key financial district, the assassination of the President of Sri Lanka, and the uncovering of an alleged conspiracy to assassinate former US President George Bush when he visited Kuwait, it is probably an understatement to claim that this volume is particularly timely.

The Editor gratefully acknowledges the assistance of the following, who made the work possible: the Research Institute for the Study of Conflict and Terrorism; University of St Andrews, and the National Strategy Information Council (NSIC), Washington, for co-sponsoring and organizing the 24–26 August 1992 seminar of experts on technology and terrorism held at St Andrews; Dr Roy Godson, Mr Tom Diaz and Mr Eric Singer of NSIC; Mr Frank Brenchley, CMG, Chairman of RISCT, who graciously chaired our sessions; Dr Myles Robertson and Mrs Gina Wilson of the St Andrews Univerity Department of International Relations for their invaluable organizational work; Randal Gray of Frank Cass for his expert copy-editing and assistance in seeing the volume through the press; and last but not least the contributors for their unfailing courtesy and commitment in preparing papers for publication in language which is comprehensible to specialists in other disciplines.

Editor's Introduction: Technology and Terrorism

PAUL WILKINSON

The role of technology is crucial to any adequate assessment of terrorism and the measures needed to combat it effectively. This was true in the late nineteenth century, the era when dynamite was the favoured weapon of groups such as Irish Fenians and French anarchists. It is even more true today in the age of Semtex and precision guided munitions (PGMs). Yet there have been very few scholarly publications, even during the recent expansion of research on terrorism, which give serious attention to the relationship between technology and terrorism.[1] The symposium that follows is a contribution towards filling this major gap. The nine studies that follow resulted from a multi-disciplinary seminar[2] involving scientists, and those with expertise in government, intelligence and law enforcement.

In this introduction my task is to identify some of the central questions about the relationship between technology and terrorism which need to be addressed. Many of these are answered in considerable detail in my colleagues' papers. My introduction will confine itself to discussing those wider themes which either went beyond the remit of the specialist contributions or emerged as recurrent themes in the informal discussions both during and following the seminar: what part has technology played in the causes of terrorism? Should it be regarded as an independent or a dependent variable in this context? Have terrorists been primarily innovative or 'conservative' in their use of technologies? Does modern technology tilt the balance in favour of the terrorists in their constant battle to defeat the efforts of the counterterrorist agencies, or vice versa? To what extent does the new technology of counterterrorism (data banks, computerised intelligence systems, etc.) threaten civil liberties? How is technology likely to affect the way terrorists in the future choose their tactics, weapons and targets?

Technology and the Causes of Terrorism

It is important to distinguish terrorism as a particular mode of violence from the specific weapons and tactics used in particular incidents or campaigns of terrorism. In essence terrorism is coercive intimidation, premeditated acts or threats of violence systemically aimed at instilling such fear in the target that it will force the target to alter its behaviour in the way desired by the terrorists.[3] Prehistoric Man probably achieved this effect by threatening to crush his victims with boulders. The medieval Assassins waged their campaign against the Sunni Muslim authorities armed with the dagger.[4] The idea of terrorism is probably as old as human history. Of course it is the case that certain key developments in technology have been of historic importance in adding new weapons to the armoury of terrorism. One such development was Alfred Nobel's invention of dynamite in 1867.[5] Nobel discovered that a porous siliceous earth, called Kieselguhr, would absorb considerable amounts of nitroglycerin. Hitherto nitroglycerin had been regarded as virtually useless owing to the absence of any reliable means for detonating it. Nobel's invention of dynamite provided a product which was relatively safe to produce and handle. By the mid-1870s Nobel had progressed to the development of gelatinous dynamites of higher density and greater plasticity producing greater blasting action power. Dynamite was seized upon by terrorists such as the Irish Fenians and the French anarchists of the Dynamite Decade, as an ideal weapon for their bombing campaigns.[6] Yet it would be as silly to blame Nobel for the rise of modern terrorism as it would to lay it at the door of the mass media or the decline of religion.

The fundamental causes of terrorism lie in the bitter ethnic, religious and ideological conflicts and hatreds which spawn such brutal violence, and the power struggles and rivalries of states.[7] It is all too evident that the ending of the Cold War, far from heralding an end of such conflicts has actually witnessed their proliferation.[8] Hence all the conditions exist in which terrorism is likely to flourish as a mode of conflict for a long time ahead, perhaps for centuries. In addition to these basic causes there are certainly other exacerbating factors which tend to make terrorism a particularly attractive and accessible method of struggle for many actors in the contemporary international system. Some of these factors are undoubtedly connected with technological developments.

First, the sheer costs and dangers of nuclear and full-scale conventional war are so huge that many state and sub-state actors see big advantages in using low-cost, low-risk, potentially high-yield methods such as terrorism as an alternative instrument of coercion. Second, the vast majority of contemporary conflicts are civil or internal wars in which the sub-state belligerents are often economically and militarily very weak, and terrorism and other forms of low-intensity conflict are often all they can manage to deploy. Third, there are many developments in modern technology which particularly lend themselves to exploitation by terrorists. For example, the development of television satellite links and global communication networks has made it easy for terrorists to relay their 'propaganda of the deed' around the world almost instantaneously. The development of light man-portable automatic weapons with a high rate of fire, portable 'fire-and-forget' missiles and malleable, highly destructive plastic explosives, like Semtex, have provided the terrorist with some powerful firepower, greatly increasing their capability of inflicting serious threats to life and property against a well-armed and sophisticated opponent.

Finally, modern technology has created new vulnerable 'key points' in all industrialized societies. One aspect of modern society which makes it far more vulnerable to terrorism is the location of vast quantities of physical energy in concentrated areas such as nuclear power stations, oil and gas storage depots and the centralization of vast quantities of information in data-processing centres and communication systems.

The list of potentially vulnerable 'key points' is so large that it would be foolish to try to include a comprehensive inventory of terrorist targets here. However, some of those most frequently attacked include: civil airports and airliners, railways, military bases and facilities, police stations, government offices, embassies and other diplomatic premises. In brief, the more economically developed and technologically sophisticated societies become, the more they inevitably present an abundance of vulnerable terrorist targets within infrastructure, central and local government, and the industrial and business sectors, for which it is simply impracticable for the authorities to provide comprehensive protection. Given the vulnerability of modern pluralistic societies to terrorist attacks, it is worth pointing out that at least one contributory indirect cause of terrorism is the failure of those governments and agencies which are likely targets to take adequate proactive and passive measures to protect themselves.

There are many experienced and cunning terrorist groups capable of seeking out the weakest links in security. Technology is clearly a vital factor in determining the level of protection appropriate to the level of threat, avoiding both under-reaction and over-reaction. But, as we shall be noting later, it is dangerous for the security authorities to be mesmerised by technology. There is no technological quick-fix to deal with terrorism. At the end of the day it is the *human* factors such as strength of will, intelligence, morale, imaginative leadership, and skills in the mobilization of public support and cooperation, which are likely to make the difference between success and failure. Technology must be an important factor in any appreciation of the problems of terrorism and counter-terrorism in modern society. Yet, it will be argued here, it must always be placed in the wider context of social, economic and political needs and problems, at national and international levels, if its role is to be properly understood.

Are Terrorists Technologically 'innovative' or 'conservative'?

Historically terrorism has very often been the weapon of the weak.[9] This has led some to assume that they are inherently backward in their use of technology or are incapable of innovation.[10] There are no firm grounds for this assumption. Within the unavoidable constraints of limited resources and lack of access to more advanced technology and expertise, many of the more experienced terrorist groups have shown considerable readiness to innovate, often improvising new weapons such as the barometric pressure bomb[11] to sabotage airliners in flight, the drogue grenade developed by the IRA described by Richard Clutterbuck (p.135), and the use of the photo-electric device to fire a bicycle bomb (as used by the Red Army Faction in Germany).

When one considers that modern terrorists have learned how to defeat the aviation authorities of numerous states, how to get prime time TV coverage,[12] and how to inflict huge damage on corporations by the use of such tactics as product contamination,[13] it would be foolish to claim that terrorists have failed to innovate. It is of course true that they have so far stopped short of using weapons of mass destruction (WMD), but we should remember that terrorist groups do not have the same access to such weapons that many states possess. And in any case it is noteworthy that even states have been reluctant to *use* such weapons, if only because of the huge political costs that might be involved. Is it any wonder that terrorist groups, most of which profess some desire to gain a political following, have also been reluctant to escalate to the level of WMD?

It is dangerously misleading to attempt to assess the relative technological sophistication of terrorist groups by comparing them with states. Governments obviously have infinitely greater financial resources, access to scientific laboratories and engineering production facilities, and whole teams of scientists and engineers to call upon in developing technology and equipment for military and security purposes. Yet this does not mean that the serious terrorist organizations are disinterested in such matters. Many make considerable efforts to obtain the services of experts in explosives, firearms, missile technology, electronics, computers, etc., to assist them in their campaigns.[14] We know that some of the major groups such as Abu Nidal's organization, the IRA, and ETA, have taken great pains to acquire technical training for their operatives.

And the richer terrorist groups have also made great efforts to obtain more advanced weapons systems and equipment from the legal and illegal arms markets, or from state sponsors.

A good example of the terrorists' proven capacity to innovate is their adoption of Semtex as a plastic explosive of choice as soon as they could obtain it from a state sponsor or other sources. Semtex is Czech-made and consists of Pentaerythrite tetranitrate combined with mineral oil as a plasticiser. It is odourless and hard to detect by vapour sniffers as it has a very low vapour pressure at normal temperature and pressure. Pentaerythrite tetranitrate is highly sensitive, but this is reduced by the mineral oil plasticiser constituent, and a powerful detonator is needed to initiate it. Semtex has a velocity of detonation of over 8000 metres per second. It is more powerful than TNT, widely in use as a military blasting explosive, which has a velocity of detonation of 7000 metres per second. Most of the energy of a Semtex bomb, is used in 'shearing' or the production of high speed fragments. From the bombers' viewpoint the main attractions of this type of plastic explosive are its enormous destructive power, and the fact that it is so malleable and easy to disguise from normal security checks. The bomb that destroyed Pan Am 103 over Lockerbie in December 1988 is believed to have been made from Semtex and concealed in a radio-cassette player. The bomb which blew up Pan Am 103 killed 270 people, 259 passengers and crew and 11 people on the ground in Lockerbie. Used in this way the terrorists' small conventional bomb became a weapon of mass destruction, causing over 40 per cent of the deaths from international terrorism in 1988.

When we bear in mind Lockerbie, the Air India disaster of 1985, and the UTA and Avianca bombings of 1989, we would be far too complacent if we were to assume that terrorists will remain wedded to weapons and tactics of limited lethality and destructive power. There is ample evidence that some terrorist groups are busy acquiring surface-to-air missiles as an alternative technology for attacking aircraft in flight.

Nor do we have to focus exclusively on the larger terrorist groups with big resources to find instances of innovation. In 1980 the French group, *Action Directe*, showed some skill and knowledge of computers when they succeeded in scientifically neutralising computers at Philips in Toulouse, causing over a quarter of a million pounds worth of damage.[15] This was the first of several attacks on computers by AD and its offshoot, Clodo, *Comité Liquidant ou Detoumant les Ordinateurs*. This is one striking example among many one could give, of the fact that even quite tiny terrorist groups have shown considerable innovation both in choice of tactics and targets.

Another important factor conducive to technological innovation by terrorists is the dynamic inherent in the constant struggle between terrorist and counter-terrorist agencies. A dramatic illustration of this process is described by Jimmie C. Oxley in her fascinating study in the present volume (pp.30–47) on 'Non-Traditional Explosives: Potential Detection Problems'. She observes:

> Present advances in explosive technology have either focused on detection of conventional military explosives or on the presence of visually recognizable components. This is an entirely reasonable approach since we have every reason to believe that terrorists will continue to use such dependable, high performance devices until we find a way to stop them . . . Unfortunately, once we have put such detectors in place, we should prepare to deal with a new generation of devices based on non-military explosives. (p.46, this volume).

Nor should we fall into the error of assuming that such innovation will inevitably involve high cost super high-technology resources on the part of the terrorists. Many of the exotic non-military explosives can be made from a combination of everyday readily-available substances. Dr Oxley warns:

> The range of explosives and the packaging possibilities is staggering. To this should also be added the incendiary devices, which might trigger a more powerful material or which, with proper placement, might prove to be every bit as devastating as an explosive. (p.46, this volume).

A lucid and thoughtful review of this technological battle from the counter-terrorism perspective is provided in Dr John Baldeschwieler's 'Explosive Detection for Commercial Aircraft Security' (pp.81–102).

Has Technology Tilted the Balance in Favour of the Terrorists?

On balance technological changes appear to have helped the terrorist far more than it has hindered him. The terrorist almost invariably has the inestimable advantage of surprise, and a huge variety of possible targets. In addition, in a democratic open society the terrorist can exploit all the freedoms of such a system all the better to attack and disrupt it. At the same time the moral, legal, and political constraints of a democratic society impose considerable restrictions on the measures and tactics available to the counter-terrorist agencies.

As Richard Clutterbuck emphasises in his contribution to this volume (pp.130–9) there have been some key developments in the field of small arms design which offer great attractions to the terrorist, such as the small, lightweight submachine-gun which combines concealment, accuracy and reliability with a high rate of fire. His analysis also rightly underlines the danger posed by new generations of man-portable precision-guided munitions (PGM).[16] The leading powers have developed a plethora of such weapons for battlefield use against tanks and aircraft. A wide range of guidance systems, ranging from radio and radar control to lasers and infra-red heat-seeking wire control, has been developed. The attractiveness of these weapons to terrorists is obvious. Some of them have a hit probability approaching one, over a range of two or three kilometres. It is true that these weapons are more costly and more difficult to steal than firearms, if only because states have tried to make it more difficult for terrorists to acquire them. Yet there have been numerous cases of terrorist groups acquiring and using surface-to-air missiles to attack aircraft. The utility of such weapons was vividly demonstrated by the mujahedin in Afghanistan. Stand-off weapons become all the more attractive to the terrorist to offset the efforts made by counter-terrorist agencies to harden potential targets such as embassies and police stations.

It is true that some technologies have been particularly valuable in counter-terrorist operations. For example, in the Northern Ireland conflict the security forces have gained immeasurably from the use of modern night-viewing devices and infra-red reconnaissance, which can reveal disturbed soil and thus locate terrorists' buried arms dumps. In many cases, however, new technologies will be exploited by *both* sides in a kind of high-tech intelligence war between terrorists and counter-terrorists. This is particularly true of highly sophisticated and experienced terrorist organizations. For example, as long ago as the 1970s the IRA had confronted the bomb disposal experts with the additional burden of dealing with sophisticated coded radio-controlled fusing systems. In the current war against the terrorists in Northern Ireland the electronic dimension has become increasingly important in surveillance, identification, detection, guidance, fusing and communications. They key to winning this kind of warfare is accurate intelligence on the capabilities of the opponent. Only when this is available is it possible to deploy appropriate countermeasures, such as jamming, deception and the whole range of electronic counter-measures (ECCM) can be utilised. This electronic intelligence war with the terrorists in Northern Ireland has become even more intense with the growing evidence of the IRA's efforts to acquire means of destroying the security forces' helicopters in flight, and to breach the security forces' security of communications.

It is because many new technologies can be exploited by *both* sides that it is so difficult to assess whether these developments have tilted the balance against the terrorists or the security forces that oppose them. This is illustrated by the impact of television as a means of mass communication. On the other hand satellite television and global news networks have provided terrorists with almost instantaneous nationwide or even world-wide publicity for their 'propaganda of the deed' and to help spread fear of further attacks among the public. Yet there is also abundant evidence that the effect of TV pictures showing the tragic effects of terrorist outrages on innocent victims can also cause a backlash of public opinion against the terrorists and can strengthen the determination of the public and the authorities to stand firm against the terrorists and to take more effective measures to combat them. For example, the IRA bombings of a shopping centre at Warrington, England, in March 1993 which caused the death of two young boys, Jonathan Ball and Tim Parry, had the effect of stirring anger and revulsion against the IRA on both sides of the Atlantic. And in Spain the TV coverage of ETA-M atrocities contributed to the largest ever anti-terrorist public demonstrations in the Basque cities. It is also important to bear in mind that TV and the print media can sometimes be of crucial value to the police in identifying and apprehending terrorist suspects. A good instance of this during the IRA bombing campaign in London in early 1993 was the use of specially enhanced pictures taken from a video-camera which led in a matter of hours to the arrest of IRA terrorists involved in a bombing outside Harrods department store and in other attacks.

In the case of technologies less widely accessible and less well-known to the public, such as the various types of sensors covering the electro-magnetic spectrum, and the use of infra-red wavelengths to detect the thermal radiation emitted by hostile sources, the main benefit has been to the security forces and those responsible for protective measures against terrorism.

Other sophisticated technologies such as the use of micro-electronics to develop computerized data bases and data processing, have the potential to provide a huge advantage to the security forces, as was well demonstrated by the German *Beobachtende Fahndung* (BEFA), the central police surveillance system, set up in the late 1970s. The computerization of massive amounts of data proved of great value to the authorities in their search for Germany's Red Army Faction terrorists because it discovered links between small pieces of information that appeared unconnected and trivial but which provided vital clues for the police hunt.

Yet computers are only a valuable tool if they are backed up by high professional ability among the police and intelligence officers, highest quality training, and effective security policy, management and procedures. It is also important to remind ourselves that the development of computer technology, and our increasing dependence on such systems in every respect of modern life, has created new vulnerabilities. For example, terrorists and organised crime gangs have been swift to learn means of sabotaging, compromising and seriously disrupting computer systems, sometimes breaching with astonishing ease, the highly inadequate computer security systems that have been developed to counter this type of crime. Nor should we forget the dangers of the 'big brother state' inherent in the trend towards increasing computerization of data of every type. It seems acceptable to many honest citizens that the police should be able to use the computer to trace a car registration number or to help apprehend terrorists on the run. But there are huge dangers involved in the potential abuse of confidential information stored in computerized data banks and the covert centralization of vast amounts of personal data at the level of government bureaucracy. If the right balance between protection against terrorism and protection of human rights is to be kept strong and effectively enforced Data Protection legislation is clearly going to be necessary. At present in the rather fragmented structure of the European Community with its ill-thought out lurch towards the dismantling of internal frontier controls, the balance is clearly tilted in favour of terrorists and others involved in major crime. In years to come this may change and it will be vital to ensure that the creation of a truly Euro-wide police and criminal justice capability is matched by adequate defences of civil liberties.

Technology and the Future of Terrorism

It was perhaps inevitable that the contributors to our symposium disagree about the future of terrorism and its likely relationship to technological developments. However, there was general agreement on three fundamental issues. First, all specialists agree that terrorism is likely to remain a major problem for many countries in the international system well into the next century. While there has been a welcome decline in the number of spectacular *international* terrorist incidents certain deeply entrenched domestic terrorist campaigns have been intensified. In early 1993 the assassination of the Sri Lankan President, the huge 24 April IRA van bomb in the City of London, and the massive casualties caused by car bombings in Bombay, were all reminders of the severe threat posed by terrorism to human rights, social well-being and the rule of law. Second, none of the specialist professes that there is a simple panacea or quick technological 'fix' that will defeat terrorism. All recognise that a multipronged response by government and society is required, and that the response must be carefully planned and calibrated according to the political context and the precise level of threat. Third, none of the experts believe in a deterministic theory of the future of terrorism, least of all a theory of technological terrorism. So much depends on the ability and will to gain the technological edge in this constantly evolving form of covert warfare.

This conflict of terrorist and counter-terrorist technology and tactics is seen in one of its most complex and deadly forms in Northern Ireland. One example on the terrorists' side is the IRA's use of a sniper team which has recently used the American-made .50-in Barrett Model 82 sniping rifle, which is accurate at more than a mile and can pierce body armour. It fires a bullet at a velocity of 1,907mph. It has a bipod stand, which gives it greater accuracy. In the year ending July 1993 the IRA sniper team killed six members of the security forces in single-shot attacks. The Barrett Light 50 is believed to have been used in at least two attacks. A top priority of the security forces in 1993 was to track down the sniper team and to capture its weaponry.

An outstanding example of technological innovation by the security forces in Northern Ireland has been set by the Explosive Ordnance Disposal (EOD) experts. For example, in 1972 they introduced the remotely-controlled tracked robot known as Wheelbarrow. This device and its later variants, proved to be one of the finest anti-bomb robot vehicles in the world. It provided a highly effective and reliable means of giving the bomb disposal officer a close-up view of a bomb without having to approach the device, and of delivering the means of neutralizing the bomb. With the aid of such devices and other techniques, courageous and dedicated bomb disposal teams in Northern Ireland have been able to prevent the death and injury of hundreds of innocent people. The full technical details as to how these successes have been achieved are only known to very few. At a time when terrorists themselves are reported to be experimenting with the development of a remotely controlled vehicle to carry a bomb to its target, it is important to be reminded that technological leadership is a crucial factor in the efforts of democratic governments and the international community confronting the challenge of increasingly sophisticated and ruthless terrorist campaigns.

NOTES

1. Honourable exceptions include the writings of Richard Clutterbuck, Brian Jenkins, Robert Kupperman, and Neil L. Livingstone.
2. The seminar was jointly organised by the Research Institute for the Study of Conflict and Terrorism and the National Strategy Information Center, and held at the University of St Andrews during 24–27 Aug. 1992. It was attended by leading government and non-government specialists in counterterrorism from the US, Western Europe and Canada.
3. For an excellent survey of the definitional issues, see Alex Schmid and Albert Jongman (eds.), *Political Terrorism: a New Guide* (Amsterdam: North Holland Publishing, 1988).
4. For fascinating account see Bernard Lewis' study *The Assassins: A Radical Sect of Islam.*
5. To this day most experts perceive Nobel's invention in 1865 of the blasting cap as a device for detonating explosives, as the greatest single advance in the science of explosives since the discovery of black gunpowder in China in the eleventh century.
6. For a general historical survey of these campaigns see Walter Laqueur, *The Age of Terrorism* (London: Weidenfeld, 1987).
7. See the discussions of the causes of terrorism in Paul Wilkinson, *Terrorism and the Liberal State*, (Basingstoke: Macmillan Education and NY: NY UP, 1986), and William Reich (ed.), *Origins of terrorism: Psychologies, ideologies, theologies, states of mind* (Cambridge and NY: W. Wilson Int'l Center for Scholars and CUP, 1990).
8. For a discussion of the implications of the ending of the Cold War for terrorism see Paul Wilkinson, *Terrorist Tactics and Targets: New Risks to World Order*, Conflict Studies, 1990.
9. This is not of course to deny that it has sometimes been the weapon of very powerful regimes, or that some sub-state organisations may become extremely well armed and well resourced relative to their opponents.
10. See, e.g., Brian Jenkins' comments that terrorists' 'tactical repertoire has changed little over time. Terrorists appear to be more imitative than innovative . . .', Brian Jenkins, 'International Terrorism: The Other World War' RAND Corp., Santa Monica, R-3302-AF (Nov. 1985), pp.12–13.
11. This type of bomb has been a particular speciality of the Palestinian extremist organisations May 15, and PFFP-GC.
12. For example, one writer has claimed that TV coverage of the 1972 Munich Olympics massacre by Black September reached an audience of around 800 millions.
13. One of the most expensive product contamination incidents ever was the lacing of Tylenol capsules in the USA. It is estimated that the total costs to the manufacturer, of Tylenol, Johnson and Johnson, resulting from the lacing of Tylenol tablets with cyanide, amounted to tens of millions, including the costs of rebuilding confidence and regaining market share, see Richard Clutterbuck (ed.), *The Future of Political Violence'* (London: Macmillan, 1986).
14. E.g., the IRA has on several occasions been caught in the US in the process of attempting to acquire sophisticated missile-systems such as Redeye and Stinger.
15. See Edward Moxon-Browne, 'Terrorism in France' in William Gutteridge (ed.) *The New Terrorism* (London: Mansell Publishing, 1986), p.131.
16. See observations by Neil Livingstone, *The War Against Terrorism* (Lexington, MA: Lexington Books, 1982), pp.108–9.

Terrorist Targeting: Tactics, Trends, and Potentialities

BRUCE HOFFMAN

This article analyzes recent trends in international terrorism in the context of tactical and technological innovation. It argues that, while terrorists were undeniably more active and considerably more lethal during the 1980s compared to the 1970s, the targets they chose, the weapons they used, and the tactics they employed remained remarkably consistent. Thus radical in their politics, the vast majority of terrorist organizations appear to be conservative in their operations, adhering largely to the same limited operational repertoire year after year. What innovation does occur is mostly in the methods used to conceal and detonate explosive devices, not in their tactics or in their use of nonconventional weapons (i.e., chemical, biological, or nuclear). If, however, terrorist lethality continues to increase and the constraints, self-imposed and otherwise, imposed on terrorists in the commission of mass murder erode further, actions involving chemical, biological, or nuclear weapons could become more attractive to some terrorist groups. Indeed, ethnic/religious fanaticism in particular might more easily allow terrorists to overcome the psychological barriers to mass murder than could a radical political agenda.

Recent trends in international terrorism present a mixed picture of change and continuity. The most salient features of these trends were the proliferation of terrorist groups and the numerous fatalities that terrorists inflicted.[1] Today, approximately 70 terrorist groups are active throughout the world. Only 11 identifiable terrorist groups were active in 1968, representing a nearly sevenfold increase in the number of terrorist organizations over the past two decades. Although the total volume of terrorist activity increased by only a third in the 1980s compared to the previous decade, terrorists killed twice as many persons.[2] This increase in lethality is reflected in the 76 per cent increase in the number of individual terrorist incidents resulting in fatalities, the 115 per cent rise in the number of incidents that caused five or more fatalities, and especially in the 135 per cent increase in the number of incidents that caused ten or more fatalities.[3] Yet, while terrorists were undeniably more active and considerably more lethal, the targets they chose, the weapons they used, and the tactics they employed remained remarkably consistent. Though superficially contradictory, this dichotomy nonetheless provides important clues toward identifying likely future patterns of terrorist targeting, tactics, and trends.

Trends in Targeting and Tactics: Innovative or Imitative?

Although terrorists killed more people during the 1980s than in the previous two decades combined, they did so without having to resort to the exotic weapons popularised by both fictional thrillers and pseudo-scholarly, headline-grabbing analysis. Bombings continued to account for roughly half of all terrorist attacks annually–as they have since 1968.[4] The reliance on bombing by terrorists is not surprising: bombs provide a dramatic, yet fairly easy and often risk-free, means of drawing attention to the terrorists and their causes. Few skills are required to manufacture a crude bomb, surreptitiously plant it, and then be miles away when it explodes. Bombs, therefore, do not require the same organizational expertise, logistics, and knowledge required of more complicated or sophisticated operations, such as kidnapping, assassination, and assaults against defended targets.

Indeed, it is not surprising to find that the frequency of various types of terrorist attacks decreases in direct proportion to the complexity or sophistication required (see Figure 1). Attacks on installations (including, for example, attacks with hand grenades, bazookas, and rocket-propelled grenades; drive-by shootings; arson; vandalism; and sabotage other than bombing), accordingly, is the second most common tactic (accounting for fewer than 20 per cent of all operations),[5] followed by assassination/shooting,[6] kidnapping, hijacking, barricade and hostage situations and significant threats variously account for the small number of remaining incidents.[7]

The fact that these percentages have remained largely unchanged for the past 25 years provides compelling evidence that the vast majority of terrorist organizations are not tactically innovative. Radical in their politics, these groups appear to be conservative in their operations, adhering largely to the same limited operational repertoire year after year. What innovation does occur is mostly in the methods used to conceal and detonate explosive devices, not in their tactics or in their use of

FIGURE 1

PER CENT OF TOTAL TERRORIST INCIDENTS BY TACTIC AND DECADE

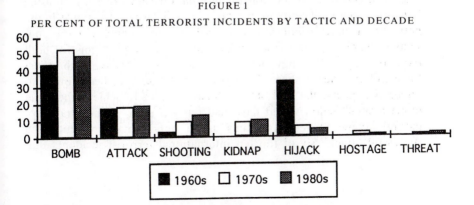

nonconventional weapons (i.e., chemical, biological, or nuclear). Terrorists continue to rely – as they have for more than a century – on the gun and the bomb: rarely do they deviate from an established *modus operandi*.

In this respect, despite its popularity as a fictional theme, terrorists have in fact rarely attempted the infliction of mass, indiscriminate casualties. Of more than 8000 incidents recorded in the RAND Chronology of International Terrorism since 1968, for example, only 52 evidence any indication of terrorist plotting such attacks or attempting to use chemical, biological, or nuclear weapons. Rather, most terrorist activity throughout the world is primarily 'symbolic', designed to call attention to the terrorists and their causes. Terrorist attacks, therefore, tend to be directed not against people, but against 'things' – such inanimate objects as embassies, consulates, government offices, businesses, military installations, and airlines that, by dint of their national identification, are replete with symbolic connotation. Thus, diplomatic targets have historically been the focus of most terrorist attacks,[8] followed by business,[9] airline,[10] military,[11] and civilian targets[12] – with attacks on energy, maritime, transportation, and communications targets comparatively rare, if not statistically insignificant. Only 20 per cent of the terrorist incidents during the 1980s, in fact, killed anyone, but those operations that did kill, as previously noted, tended to kill more people than before. The reasons that explain this trend – the terrorists' apparent belief that lethality attracts attention; improved effectiveness of terrorist organizations over generations; the resurgence of religious terrorism; the fact that terrorists themselves are more adept at killing; and increased state-sponsorship of terrorism – also shed light on terrorist capabilities, targeting, tactics, and decision making.

International Terrorism's Increasing Lethality

The most obvious explanation for international terrorism's increasing lethality is that public attention is not as readily aroused as it was in the past. The general proliferation of terrorist movements and the consequent increase in terrorist incidents have created problems for both old and – especially – new groups who now must compete with others for a wider audience share.[13] Terrorists have therefore been forced to undertake spectacular and bloody deeds in order to achieve the same effect a small action would have had ten years ago[14] – and have apparently come to regard victims as an important ingredient of a successful attack. Six of the ten international terrorist incidents that have caused the greatest number of fatalities since 1968, for example, have occurred within the last nine years. A Tamil separatist group in Sri Lanka, the Liberation Tigers of Tamil Eelam, is a specific case in point. Although the group was formed in 1972 and commenced terrorist operations three years later, the Liberation Tigers went largely unnoticed outside of Sri Lanka until 1986, when a bomb placed aboard a Sri Lankan airliner delayed at Colombo International Airport killed 21 persons and wounded 40 others – many of whom were foreign nationals. The large number of casualties involving foreign nationals assured the terrorists the international attention and notoriety that their campaign exclusively against Sri Lankan targets had lacked.

Other terrorist acts are not only driven by the desire for publicity but are explicitly coercive as well, threatening dire consequences unless specific demands are met. The wave of bombings that shook Paris during 1986 – beginning in February with an explosion in a shopping centre that killed eight persons and culminating the following September with a nine-day terrorist rampage that killed another eight persons and wounded more than 150 others – is an example of this symbiosis of objectives. Following the first incident, a group calling itself the Committee of Solidarity with the Arab and Middle East Political Prisoners claimed credit for the bombing and demanded the release of three terrorists imprisoned in France. After the French government refused to accede to this demand, three more bombings occurred in February, two more the following month, and five in September.

Still other terrorist operations are purportedly carried out in reprisal for or to call attention to a particular government's actions. In this category is the September 1986 attack on an Istanbul synagogue that claimed the lives of 22 people and wounded three others. Two members of the Abu Nidal Organization threw hand grenades and machine-gunned the worshippers attending sabbath services, before dousing their victims' bodies with gasoline and attempting to set them afire. A spokesman in Beirut later claimed that the operation had been staged in retaliation for a recent Israeli raid on a guerrilla base in southern Lebanon.

An almost Darwinian principle of natural selection also seems to affect all terrorist groups, so that every new terrorist generation learns from its predecessors, becoming smarter, tougher, and more difficult to capture or eliminate.[15] For terrorists, intelligence is not only an essential prerequisite for a successful operation, but a *sine qua non* for survival. Successor generations, therefore, routinely study the 'lessons' from mistakes made by former comrades who have been either killed or apprehended. Press accounts, judicial indictments, courtroom testimony, and trial transcripts are meticulously culled for information on security force tactics and methods and absorbed by surviving group members.[16]

Not only are successor generations smarter than their predecessors, but they also tend to be more ruthless and less idealistic. For some, in fact, violence becomes almost an end in itself – a cathartic release, a self-satisfying blow struck against the hated 'system' – rather than being regarded as the deliberate means to a specific political end embraced by previous generations.[17] A dedicated, 'hard-core' of some 20 to 30 terrorists today, for example, compose a third generation of Germany's Red Army Faction (RAF) terrorist organization. In contrast to the group's first generation, who more than twenty years ago embarked on an anti-establishment campaign of non-lethal bombings and arson attacks, the present generation – at least until recently[18] – has pursued a strategy of cold-blooded assassination.

During the past five years, the Red Army Faction has murdered six prominent – and heavily guarded – Germans. The last victim was Detlev Rohwedder, a wealthy industrialist and chairman of the *Treuhandanstalt*, or Public Trustee, the government agency charged with overseeing the economic transition of eastern Germany. Rohwedder was killed in April 1991, by a shot fired from a high-power rifle while he sat in his study.[19] In December 1989 financier and Deutsche Bank president Alfred Herrhausen was assassinated when a state-of-the-art remote-control bomb, concealed in a parked bicycle and triggered by a light-beam, was detonated just as Herrhausen's car passed. A similar device was used the following July in an attempt to assassinate Germany's top government counter-terrorist official, Hans Neusel.[20]

Almost as disturbing as the assassinations themselves is the fact that the perpetrators – and their fellow conspirators – have eluded what is perhaps the most sophisticated anti-terrorist machinery in the world. 'The "Third Generation" learnt a lot from the mistakes of its predecessors–and about how the police works', a spokesperson for the *Bundeskriminalamt* lamented in 1991, 'they now know how to operate very carefully.'[20] Indeed, according to a former member of the organization, Peter-Juergen Brock, currently serving the eighth year of a life sentence for murder, the group 'has reached maximum efficiency'.[22]

Another key reason for terrorism's increased lethality is the growing incidence of violence motivated by a religious, as well as a nationalist/separatist imperative.[23] Certainly, the relationship between terrorism and religion is not new. In fact, as David C. Rapoport points out in his seminal study of what he terms 'holy terror', until the nineteenth century, 'religion provided the only acceptable justifications for terror.'[24] This form of terrorism has occurred throughout history, although in recent decades it has largely been overshadowed by nationalist/separatist or ideologically motivated terrorism.[25]

The record of terrorist acts by Shi'a Islamic groups reinforces, for example, the causal link between religion-motivated terrorism and terrorism's growing lethality. Although these groups have committed only 8 per cent of all international terrorist incidents since 1982, they are responsible for 30 per cent of the total number of deaths.[26] Moreover, contrary to its depiction and discussion in Western news accounts, terrorism motivated by religion is by no means a phenomenon restricted to Islamic terrorist groups exclusively in the Middle East. Many of the characteristics of Shi'a terrorist groups – the legitimization of violence based on religious precepts, the sense of alienation, the existence of a terrorist movement in which the activists are the constituents, and preoccupation with the elimination of a broadly defined category of 'enemies' – are also apparent among militant Christian white supremacists in the United States and in at least some radical Jewish messianic terrorist movements in Israel.

The elimination of whole segments of society is in fact a major objective of the white supremacists and, in at least one major incident, was partly the aim of the Jewish terrorists. Both groups view violence as morally justified and as an expedient toward the attainment of the religious and racial 'purification' of their respective countries.[27] In 1987, for example, 14 American white supremacists were indicted on federal charges of plotting to engage in indiscriminate, mass killing through the poisoning of municipal water supplies in two major American cities.[28] Similarly, in 1984, two separate groups of Israeli religious fanatics were convicted of plotting to blow up the Dome of the Rock in Jerusalem, Islam's third holiest shrine, in part to provoke a cataclysmic holy war between Muslims and Jews that would force the Jewish Messiah to intervene.[29]

That terrorists motivated by a religious imperative can contemplate such massive acts of death is a reflection of their belief that violence is a sacramental act or a divine duty. Terrorism thus assumes a transcendental dimension,[30] and its perpetrators are unconstrained by the political, moral, or practical constraints that affect other terrorists. Whereas secular terrorists generally consider indiscriminate violence immoral and counterproductive,[31] religious terrorists regard such violence as both morally justified and expedient for the attainment of their goals.

Religious and secular terrorists also differ in their constituencies. Religious terrorists are at once activists and constituents engaged in what they regard as a 'total war'. They perform their terrorist acts for no audience but themselves. Thus the restraints on violence that are imposed on secular terrorists by the desire to appeal to an uncommitted constituency are not relevant to the religious terrorist. Finally, religious and secular terrorists have different perceptions of themselves and their violent acts. Secular terrorists regard violence as a way of instigating the correction of a flaw in a system that is basically good or to foment the creation of a new system. Religious terrorists, on the other hand, regard themselves not as components of a system, but as 'outsiders', and seek vast changes in the existing order.[32] This sense of alienation enables the religious terrorist to contemplate far more destructive and deadly types of terrorist operations than secular terrorists and indeed to embrace a far more open-ended category of 'enemies' for attack.

Terrorism's trend toward increasing lethality is also a reflection of the fact that terrorists themselves are more adept at killing.[33] Not only are their weapons becoming smaller, more sophisticated,[34] and deadlier–as exemplified by the time bomb, constructed from less than 300 grams of Czech-manufactured plastic explosive[35] that was hidden inside a radio cassette player and is believed to have brought down Pan Am Flight 103 over Lockerbie in December 1988 – but terrorists have greater access to these weapons through their alliance with foreign governments.

In addition to their standard arsenal of small arms and ordinary explosives, various 'state-sponsored' terrorists respectively used a truck carrying a bomb consisting of some 12,000 pounds of high explosives, whose destructive power was enhanced by canisters of flammable gases, to kill 241 US Marines in what has been described as the 'largest non-nuclear blast ever detonated on the face of the earth', [36] deployed nearly 200 sophisticated, multifused, Soviet-manufactured acoustic naval mines to disrupt shipping entering the Suez Canal from the Red Sea; carried out a coordinated car-bomb attack in the Karachi commercial district that killed 72 persons and wounded more that 250 others; and fabricated the device that exploded aboard Pan Am Flight 103 killing all 259 on board as well as 11 others on the ground. It is not surprising, therefore, to find that state-sponsored terrorist incidents are, on average, eight times more lethal than those carried out by groups acting on their own.[37]

Admittedly, diminishing communist-bloc support and training of various international terrorist organisations will make it more difficult for those groups to operate.[38] However, recent reports that during the past decade Czechoslovakia shipped more than 1,000 *tons* of Semtex plastic explosive (the same type used against Pan Am 103) to Libya ensure that at least those terrorist organisations still favoured by Colonel Gaddafi[39] will have ample supplies of that explosive for years to come.[40] Moreover, in addition to the Libyan shipments, Czechoslovakia is also reported to have exported some 40,000 tons of Semtex to Syria, North Korea, Iran and Iraq – countries long cited by the US Department of State as sponsors of international terrorist activity. Accordingly, irrespective of communist-bloc action, terrorists now are assured an almost inexhaustible international stockpile of plastic explosives on which to draw for future operations.[41] Moreover, even those organisations lacking a government patron or sponsor can easily obtain a range of sophisticated weapons – including Semtex-H – on the international black market.[42]

The Struggle for Technological Superiority

The availability of these weapons coupled with the terrorists' own operational ingenuity has enabled at least some groups to stay constantly ahead of the counter-terrorist technology curve and repeatedly frustrate or defeat the security measures placed in their path. Relying on unconventional adaptations or modifications to conventional explosive devices, these organisations have been able to develop innovative and devastatingly effective means to conceal, deliver, and detonate all kinds of bombs. The devices used respectively in the aforementioned assassination of Alfred Herrhausen and the downing of Pan Am Flight 103 are two examples where terrorists used specially or cleverly modified 'off-the-shelf' technology to strike at two purportedly well-defended targets.[43] The one-eighth of an inch thick, four-inch wide, and ten-inch long bomb, constructed of 300 grams of Semtex and triggered by a combination of electronic timer and barometric sensor, that was placed under the seat cushion of a TWA flight en route from Cairo to Athens via Rome and exploded killing four persons and injuring nine others in April 1986,[44] and the liquid explosive concealed in a generic half-gallon whisky bottle placed in an overhead bin during a Korean Air flight in November 1987 and detonated nine hours later by 12 ounces of C-4 plastic explosive wired to a timing device hidden in a transistor radio placed in the seatpocket below, killing all 115 persons on board, are two other chilling examples of terrorist creativity and adaptation.[45]

The PIRA's relentless quest to pierce the armour protecting both the security forces in Northern Ireland and the most senior government officials in Britain illustrates the dynamics of this struggle for technological superiority. The first generation of early 1970s PIRA devices were often little more than crude anti-personnel bombs, consisting of a handful of roofing nails wrapped around a lump of plastic explosive, that were detonated simply by lighting a fuse. Time bombs from the same era were hardly more sophisticated. They typically were constructed from a few

sticks of dynamite and commercial detonators stolen from construction
sites or rock quarries attached to ordinary battery-powered alarm
clocks. Neither device was terribly reliable and often put the bomber at
considerable risk. The process of placing and actually lighting the first
type of device carried with it the inherent potential to attract undesired
attention while affording the bomber little time to effect the attack and
make good his or her escape. Although the second type of device was
designed to mitigate precisely this danger, its timing and detonation
mechanism was often so crude that accidental or premature explosions
were not infrequent, resulting in some accidental terrorist deaths.[46]

In hopes of obviating, or at least reducing, these risks, the PIRA's
bombmakers invented a means of detonating bombs from a safe distance using the radio controls of model aircraft purchased at hobby
shops. Scientists and engineers working in the British Ministry of
Defence's (MoD) scientific research and development (R&D) division
in turn developed a system of electronic countermeasures and jamming
techniques for the Army that effectively thwarted this means of attack.[47]
However, rather than abandon this tactic completely, the PIRA began
to search for a solution. In contrast to the state-of-the art laboratories,
huge budgets, and academic credentials of their government counterparts, PIRA's own 'R&D' department toiled in cellars beneath
cross-border safehouses and backrooms of urban tenements for five
years before devising a network of sophisticated electronic switches for
their bombs that would ignore or bypass the Army's electronic counter-
measures.[48]

Once again, the MoD scientists returned to their laboratories, emerging with a new system of electronic scanners able to detect radio
emissions the moment the radio is switched on – and, critically, just
tenths of seconds before the bomber can actually transmit the detonation signal. The almost infinitesimal window of time provided by this
'early warning' of impending attack is just sufficient to allow Army tech-
nicians to activate a series of additional electronic measures to
neutralize the transmission signal and render detonation impossible. For
a time, this countermeasure proved effective, as well. But by 1991, the
PIRA had discovered a means to outwit even this countermeasure. Uti-
lizing radar detectors, such as those used by motorists in the United
States to avoid speed traps, the group's bombmakers fabricated a detonating system that can be triggered by the same type of hand-held
radar gun used by police throughout the world to catch speeding
motorists. Since the radar gun can be aimed at its target before being
switched on, and the signal that it transmits is nearly instantaneous, no
practical means currently exists to detect or intercept the transmission
signal in time.[49]

Even attacks that are not successful in conventionally understood military terms can still be a success for the terrorists provided that they are technologically daring enough to garner media and public attention. Indeed, the terrorist group's fundamental organizational imperative to act – even if their action is not completely successful but still brings them publicity – also drives this persistent search for new ways to overcome, circumvent or defeat governmental security and countermeasures. Thus, while the PIRA failed to kill then-Prime Minister Margaret Thatcher in October 1984 at the Conservative Party's annual conference in Brighton, the technological ingenuity involving the bomb's placement at the conference site weeks before the event and its detonation timing device powered by a computer mircochip nonetheless succeeded in capturing the world's headlines and provided the PIRA with a platform from which to warn Mrs Thatcher and all other British leaders: 'Today we were unlucky, but remember we only have to be lucky once – you will have to be lucky always.'[50] Similarly, although the remote-control mortar attack staged by the PIRA on No. 10 Downing Street – as Prime Minister John Major and his Cabinet met in the midst of the 1991 Gulf War – failed to hit its intended target, the attack nonetheless successfully elbowed the war out of the limelight and shone renewed media attention on the terrorists, their cause, and their impressive ability to strike at the nerve centre of the British government even at a time of heightened security.[51]

Although the technological mastery employed by the PIRA is arguably unique among terrorist organisations, experience has nonetheless demonstrated repeatedly that, when confronted by new security measures, terrorists throughout the world often will seek to identify and exploit new vulnerabilities, adjusting their means of attack accordingly.[52] This point is especially pertinent to the threat posed by terrorists to commercial aviation. During the late 1960s, for example, hijacking of passenger aircraft was among terrorists' favoured tactics, accounting for 33 per cent of all incidents (see Figure 1). However, as security at airports improved, as metal detectors and x-ray machines were installed at boarding areas, and as passenger profiling and other countermeasures were adopted, the incidence of airline hijackings declined appreciably to just 7 per cent of all incidents in the 1970s and only 4 per cent in the 1980s. While these measures were successful in reducing airline hijackings, they did not stop terrorist attacks on commercial airlines altogether. Instead, prevented from smuggling weapons on board to hijack aircraft, terrorists merely continued to attack them by means of bombs hidden in carry-on or checked baggage.

Admittedly, a new generation of sophisticated bomb detection devices – able to detect even plastic explosives – are currently being installed at airports throughout the world, while a successor generation involving other techniques is already being tested. These machines, using thermal neutron activation methods, gamma ray resonance techniques, etc., will doubtlessly make it still more difficult for terrorists to place bombs on board aircraft in much the same way as the metal detectors and x-ray machines made hijacking more difficult. But if past experience is any guide, as airport security and bomb detection technology closes off this avenue of attack, terrorists will not give up attacking airliners but merely find another means of doing so. They are likely to turn to readily available shoulder-fired, precision-guided surface-to-air missiles as the only practical means to attack commercial aircraft. A single terrorist, trained in the use of this weapon, could position himself at the edge of any airport's runway and fire at incoming or departing passenger planes.

Indeed, on the few occasions in the past when guerrillas have targeted nonmilitary aircraft with surface-to-air missiles, they have had spectacularly devastating results. Black nationalist guerrillas downed two Rhodesian passenger jets with SAM-7s in 1978 and 1979, killing a total of 107 persons. Sudanese rebels used a SAM-7 in 1986 to shoot down a Sudan Airways commercial jet, killing all 60 persons on board. And, Polisario Front guerrillas in Morocco downed an American DC-7 weather plane in 1988 with a Soviet missile, killing its five-man crew.[53] The proven effectiveness of such weapons has reportedly led the British Army to respond to alleged PIRA possession of Libyan-supplied SAM-7s[54] by equipping its helicopters in Northern Ireland with infrared defensive systems – described as 'the most sophisticated anti-missile systems in use by the North Atlantic Treaty Organization Forces in Europe' – to thwart missile attacks.[55] Given the fact that the arsenals of some 80 countries throughout the world now contain SAM-7s – or their non-communist bloc equivalents – that countries as diverse as Egypt, China, Brazil, South Africa, and Sweden are at various stages of producing their own manportable surface-to-air missiles,[56] and that such weapons can reputedly be purchased on the international arms 'black market' for as little as $80,000, terrorist and guerrilla use of these weapons is likely to increase in the future.[57]

Conclusion: Some Thoughts on Likely Future Terrorist Tactics and Targets

Most analyses of the possibility of chemical, biological, or nuclear terrorism have tended to discount it because few terrorists know anything about the technical intricacies of either developing or dispersing such weapons, and the internal dynamics and decision-making processes of terrorist groups tend to inhibit sudden escalations or changes in either tactics or level of violence. Political, moral, and practical considerations also affect terrorist decision-making. There are few realistic demands that terrorists could make by threatening the use of such indiscriminate weapons. More important, as Brian Jenkins notes, 'simply killing a lot of people has seldom been one terrorist objective . . . Terrorists operate on the principle of the minimum force necessary. They find it unnecessary to kill many, as long as killing a few suffices for their purposes.'[58] Terrorists have demonstrated repeatedly that their goals and objectives can be accomplished by using the same tactics and 'off-the-shelf weapons' (though cleverly modified or adapted to their needs) that they have traditionally relied upon.

These arguments are supported by the general pattern of worldwide terrorism. Bombing continues to account for the majority of terrorist operations, and most of the bombs are not particularly innovative. Most are made of commercially purchased or stolen dynamite or from plastic explosives procured or stolen from military stockpiles. Even those instances involving comparatively more sophisticated, state-sponsored, terrorists, the weapons used have been exclusively conventional.

If, however, terrorist lethality continues to increase and the constraints, self-imposed and otherwise imposed on terrorists in the commission of mass murder erode further, actions involving chemical, biological, or nuclear weapons could become more attractive to some terrorist groups. However, in this respect it should be emphasised that terrorists have yet to reach their killing potential using even 'off-the-shelf' weapons. Terrorists, moreover, have generally kept their threats 'realistic' (in the sense that they can and will carry these threats out if denied their objectives) and approximately commensurate with the demands made. Any use of chemical, biological, or nuclear weapons could result in unprecedented numbers of casualties and damage, with attendant undesired (by the terrorists) implications for public opinion and government reaction. Also, as previously noted, the terrorists' traditional arsenal of the bomb and the gun still suffice to exact or win from governments the concessions that terrorists typically seek.

Today, however, when old empires and countries are crumbling and new ones are being built, the possession of a nuclear bomb or the development of a chemical or biological warfare capability may become increasingly attractive either to new nations seeking to preserve their sovereignty or to would-be nations seeking to attain their independence.

In both instances, terrorists may find new roles for their skills and expertise. Terrorists may be employed by countries either to steal nuclear
weapons or strategic material from another country or to stage a covert
nuclear, chemical, or biological attack in order to conceal the involvement or complicity of their state patron. In this respect, the lesson of
Iraq's overt invasion of Kuwait looms large. In the future, terrorists may
become the 'ultimate fifth column': a clandestine, cost-effective force
used to wage war covertly against more powerful rivals or to subvert
neighbouring countries or hostile regimes.

By the same token, ethnic/religious fanaticism could more easily
allow terrorists to overcome the psychological barriers to mass murder
than could a radical political agenda. A terrorist group of religious zea-
lots, with state support, in a context of ongoing violence (i.e., the civil
war in Yugloslavia or some new internecine conflict in one of the former
Soviet Union's republics) could see the acquisition and use of a chemical, biological, or nuclear capability a viable option. State sponsorship,
in particular, could provide terrorists with the incentives, capabilities,
and resources they previously lacked for undertaking an ambitious operation in any of these domains. Combined with intense ethnic enmity or a
strong religious imperative, this could prove deadly.[59]

One final observation seems in order: while the volume of worldwide
terrorism fluctuates from year to year, one enduring feature is that
Americans remain favoured targets of terrorists abroad. Since 1968 the
United States has annually headed the list of countries whose nationals
and property are most frequently attacked by terrorists.[60] This is a
phenomenon attributable as much to the geographical scope and diver-
sity of America's overseas commercial interests and its numerous
military bases on foreign soil as to the United States' stature as a super-
power and leader of the free world. Terrorists, therefore, are attracted
to American interests' and citizens abroad precisely because of the
plethora of readily available targets; the terrorists' perceived difficulty
of operating and striking targets in the United States itself; the symbolic
value inherent in any blow struck against US 'expansionism', 'im-
perialism', or 'economic exploitation', and, not least, because of the
unparalleled opportunities for exposure and publicity from perhaps the
world's most extensive news media that any attack on an American target – especially one that involves civilian casualties – assures. These
reasons suggest that, despite the end of both the Cold War and the ideological polarization that divided the world, the United States will
nonetheless remain an attractive target for terrorists seeking to attract
attention to themselves and their causes. Moreover, as the only super-
power, the United States may likely be blamed for more of the world's ills
– and therefore could be the focus of more terrorist attacks – than before.[61]

NOTES

1. Paper presented at the 'Seminar on Technology and Terrorism', at the University of St Andrews, Scotland, 24–27 Aug. 1992. The author also wishes to acknowledge the helpful comments provided by Jennifer Morrison Taw of the RAND research staff.
2. According to The RAND Chronology of International Terrorism, 2536 incidents occurred between 1970 and 1979, compared to 3658 between 1980 and 1989; a total of 4077 persons were killed by terrorists between 1980 and 1989, compared to the 1975 killed between 1970 and 1979.
3. Unless otherwise noted, the statistics presented in this paper are derived from The RAND Chronology of International Terrorism.
4. Forty-nine per cent of all terrorist attacks in the 1980s involved bombings, 53 per cent in the 1970s, and, 44 per cent in 1968/69.
5. Nineteen per cent in the 1980s and 1970s and 18 per cent in 1968/69.
6. Thirteen per cent in the 1980s, nine per cent in the 1970s, and only three per cent in 1968/69.
7. Kidnappings accounted for 10 per cent of all terrorist attacks in the 1980s, 9 per cent in the 1970s, and just .01% in 1968/69, hijackings for 4 per cent of the incidents in the 1980s, 7 per cent in the 1970s, and, 33 per cent in 1968/69, and barricade and hostage situations for just 1 per cent in the 1980s, 3 per cent in the 1970s, and none in 1968/69.
8. Accounting for 23 per cent of terrorist operations in the 1980s, 29 per cent in the 1970s, and 32 per cent in 1968/69.
9. Twenty-one per cent of terrorist operations in the 1980s and 1970s, and 14 per cent in the 1970s.
10. Twelve per cent of terrorist operations in the 1980s, 21 per cent in the 1970s, and 38 per cent in the 1968/69.
11. Ten per cent of terrorist operations in the 1980s, seven per cent in the 1970s, and .03 per cent in 1968/69.
12. Nine per cent of terrorist attacks in the 1980s, eight per cent in the 1970s, and, none in 1968/69.
13. The intensification of violence in Spain during the months prior to the 1992 Barcelona Olympic Games by the Basque separatist group, ETA, where attacks became considerably more indiscriminate (i.e., involving the use of large car bombs), is one example. See Adela Gooch, 'Eta bomb suspects killed in police raid', Independent (London), 31 May 1991; Francisco D. Galvez Cantero, 'ETA Targets 1992 Olympics', Conflict International 6/1 (May 1991); and Adela Gooch, 'Eta and Madrid engaged in a battle of nerves', Independent (London), 31 Jan. 1992.
14. See e.g., David Hearts, 'Publicity key element of strategy', Guardian (London), 31 July 1990; and David Pallister, 'Provos seek to "play havoc with British nerves and lifestyle,"' Guardian (London), 31 July 1990.
15. See, e.g., the discussion of Germany's Red Army Faction in Peter Schere, 'RAF Concentrates on New Target Spectrum', Die Welt (Hamburg), 18 Dec. 1991.
16. According to one German government official, terrorists belonging to the Red Army Faction (RAF) 'closely study every court case against them to discover their weak spots'. Whereas in the past, police could usually obtain fingerprints from the bottom of toilet seats or the inside of refrigerators, RAF terrorists today apply a special ointment to their fingers that, after drying prevents fingerprints. See Frederick Kempe, 'Deadly Survivors: The Cold War Is Over But Leftist Terrorists In Germany Fight On'. Wall Street Journal, 27 Dec. 1991. The Provisional Irish Republican Army (PIRA) was recently described by a high-ranking British Army officer serving in Northern Ireland as 'better equipped, better resourced, better led, bolder and more secure against our penetration than at any time before. They are an absolutely formidable enemy. The essential attributes of their leaders are better than ever before. Some of their operations are brilliant in terrorist terms.' Quoted in Edward Gorman, 'How to stop the IRA', The Times (London), 11 Jan. 1992. A similar observation is made by a Royal Ulster Constabulary spokesman in the province who noted that

even the PIRA's relatively unsophisticated Protestant terrorist counterparts, '[m]ore and more . . . are running their operations from small cells, on a need to know basis. They have cracked down on loose talk. They have learned how to destroy forensic evidence. And if your bring them in for questioning, they say nothing.' Quoted in William E. Schmidt, 'Protestant Gunmen Are Stepping Up the Violence in Northern Ireland', *New York Times* 29 Oct. 1991.

17.   Ibid.

18.   In April and June 1992 the RAF issued communiqués offering to suspend its terrorist campaign provided various conditions – mostly involving the release of imprisoned RAF terrorists – were met by the German government. For a detailed analysis of both the RAF and the two communiqués, see Dennis A. Pluchinsky, 'Germany's Red Army Faction: An Obituary', *Studies in Conflict and Terrorism* 16/2 (Summer 1993).

19.   Adrian Bridge, 'German police search for Red Army Faction killers', *Independent* (London), 6 April 1991; Stephen Kinzer, 'Red Army Faction Is suspected in German Killings', *New York Times*, 3 April 1991; and Bernard Adamczewski, 'United Germany Divided by Terror', *Conflict International* 6/3 (1991), p.1.

20.   'Bonn's top terror expert survives bomb', *Independent* (London), 28 July 1990; and Ian Murray, 'German police chief survives car bomb,' *The Times* (London), 28 July 1990. As one German federal investigator observed: 'When the RAF kills, it usually gets the sort of people who are impossible to replace', (quoted in Kempe, 'Deadly Survivors: The Cold War Is Over But Leftist Terrorists In Germany Fight On', *Wall Street Journal*, 27 Dec. 1991).

21.   Quoted in Adrian Bridge, 'German police search for Red Army Faction Killers,' *Independent* (London), 6 April 1991.

22.   Quoted in Kempe, 'Deadly Survivors: The Cold War Is Over But Leftist Terrorists In Germany Fight On', *Wall Street Journal*, 27 Dec. 1991.

23.   For a more detailed discussion of these distinctions see the author's 'The Contrasting Ethical Foundations of Terrorism in the 1980s' in *Terrorism and Political Violence* 1/3 (July 1989), pp.361–77. This article was also published under the same title in Jan. 1988 in the RAND Paper series as P-7416.

24.   David C. Rapoport, 'Fear and Trembling: Terrorism in Three Religious Traditions', *American Political Science Review* 78/3 (Sept. 1984), p.659.

25.   For example, none of the identifiable terrorist groups active in 1969 could be classified as 'religious'. By 1989, however, at least 12 groups had a dominant religious component. Admittedly many 'secular' terrorist groups have a strong religious element as well (e.g., the PIRA, the Armenians, and perhaps the PLO). However, the political aspect is the predominant characteristic of these groups, as evinced by their nationalist or irredentist aims.

26.   According to The RAND Chronology of International Terrorism between 1982 and 1989 Shi'a terrorist groups committed 247 terrorist incidents but were responsible for 1057 deaths.

27.   Significantly, both the white supremacist and Jewish campaigns were approved by their respective religious authorities. For the theological justification of the white supremacist campaign see such movement publications as, Aryan Nations , *Calling Our Nation*, No.53 (n.d.), p.2 and 'To Our New People', Open Letter from Richard G. Butler, Pastor, Aryan Nations, (n.d.); and for the Jewish campaign see the detailed scholarly analysis in Ehud Sprinzak, *The Ascendance of Israel's Radical Right* (NY and Oxford: OUP, 1991), pp.98–9. Specifically, Sprinzak notes that the 'rabbinical involvement in the terror acts that did and did not take place is of crucial importance. It tells us that the radicalization process that finally produced terrorism with Gush Emunim [the radical Israeli settlers' movement from which the terrorists came] was not marginal but central . . . [moreover] a combination of messianic belief and a situation of continual national conflict with a built-in propensity for incremental violence resulted in extralegalism, vigilantism, selective terrorism, and finally, *indiscriminate mass terrorism* [my emphasis].'

28.   See *Arkansas Gazette* (Little Rock Arkansas), 27 April 1987 cited in Bruce Hoffman,

Recent Trends and Future Prospects of Terrorism in the United States (Santa Monica, CA: RAND Corp. R-3618, May 1988), p.61

29. Information provided to the author by an American law enforcement official. See also, Thomas L. Friedman, 'Jewish Terrorists Freed by Israel', *New York Times*, 9 Dec. 1984; Grace Halsell, 'Why Bobby Brown of Brooklyn wants to blow up Al Aqsa'. *Arabia*, Aug. 1984; Martin Merzer, 'Justice for all in Israel?' *Miami Herald*, 17 May 1985; and 'Jail Term of Jewish terrorist reduced', *Jerusalem Post* 12 Oct. 1985. The terrorists' desire to provoke a cataclysmic holy war between Muslims and Jews was verified by an American law enforcement officer investigating Jewish terrorist incidents in the US and knowledgeable of the Jerusalem incident. For a detailed account of both the Temple Mount 'plot' and Jewish terrorist attacks on Arab targets in Israel during 1983 and 1984, see Sprinzak, *Ascendance of Israel's Radical Right*, pp.98–9.

30. See, e.g., Rapoport, 'Fear and Trembling: Terrorism in Three Religious Traditions', p.674.

31. Brian M. Jenkins, *The Likelihood of Nuclear Terrorism* (Santa Monica, CA: RAND, July 1985, P-7119),pp.4–5.

32. See, e.g., Amir Taheri, *Holy Terror: The Inside Story of Islamic Terrorism* (London: Sphere Books, 1987), pp.7–8.

33. The PIRA, for example, has been described by one senior British security official as 'Without doubt . . . the most professional terrorist organisation in the world today', James Adams and Liam Clarke, 'War Without End', *Sunday Times* (London), 27 June, 1990.

34. See, e.g., David Rose, 'Devices reveal IRA know-how', *Guardian* (London) 28 May, 1990.

35. Discussion with US airline official with particular knowledge of the Pan Am 103 bombing. Eight ounces (224g) is the amount of plastic explosive that the new thermal neutron analysis devices are calibrated to detect. See 'Explosive Detection Systems Boosted, Blasted at Hearing', *Counter-Terrorism and Security Intelligence*, 12 Feb. 1990.

35. Eric Hammel, *The Root: The Marines in Beirut, August 1982–February 1984* (San Diego, CA; Harcourt Brace Jovanovich, 1985), p.303.

37. Statistic deduced based on information from The RAND Chronology of International Terrorism.

38. Czech President Vaclav Havel, for example, banned the export of Semtex in early 1990. See John Tagliabue, 'Arms Exports Bring Profits and Pain To Czechs and Especially to Slovaks', *New York Times*, 19 Feb. 1992. Documents recently obtained from the Soviet Union Communist Party archive detail Soviet help for Palestinian terrorist groups during the 1970s. See Serge Schemann, 'Soviets Gave Arms to Palestine Band', *New York Times*, 26 May 1992. Indeed, according to Amos Gilboa, a former deputy head of Israeli military intelligence, some 5,000 members of various Palestinian terrorist organizations have been trained since 1973 in east bloc countries such as East Germany, Romania, Poland, Hungary, and Czechoslovakia. See Ian Black, 'East European reforms cut off sources of aid to PLO', *Guardian*, 22 Jan. 1990. In addition, the arrests in East Germany–and extraditions to West Germany before reunification–of nine leading Red Army Faction terrorists, based on information apparently furnished by a disgruntled former agent in the East German state security organization, was further evidence that the sanctuary previously enjoyed by terrorists behind the Iron Curtain had ended. See 'East Germans Seize 4 Tied to Terror in West', *New York Times*, 16 June 1990; 'Bonn Links Woman Held in East to Killings of GIs,' *New York Times*, 17 June 1990; 'Terrorists left without a curtain', *Washington Times*, 18 June 1990; 'East Germans Hold Two More Suspects In Terrorist Attacks', *New York Times*, 20 June 1990; 'Stasi connection beckons in German terrorist trial', *Guardian* (London), 4 May 1990; and Anna Tomforde, 'German terrorist gets 12 years', *Guardian* (London), 4 June 1991.

39. Among the groups believed to have already benefited from Libya's largesse include:

PIRA, PFLP General Command, the Lebanese Armed Revolutionary Faction (LARF), the Armenian Secret Army for the Liberation of Armenia (ASALA), the Palestinian May 15th Organization, the elite Force-17 unit of *al-Fatah*, the renegade Palestinian Abu Nidal Organization, and the Italian Red Brigades. See 'Czechoslovakia and the Middle East: A New Ball Game', MEDNEWS (*Middle Eastern Defense News*) 30 April, 1990, p5; and Glenn Frankel, 'Sale of Explosives to Libya Detailed' *Washington Post*, 23 March 1990. As previously noted the PIRA allegedly received five to ten tons of Semtex from Libya in addition to another 120 tons of arms and explosives, including 12 SAM-7 ground-to-air missiles. 'IRA: The Libyan Connection', *The Economist*, 31 March 1990.

40. As Czech president, Vaclav Havel observed on an official visit to Britain: 'If you consider that 200 grams is enough to blow up an aircraft . . . this means world terrorism has enough Semtex to last 150 years.' Quoted in Glenn Frankel, 'Sale of Explosive to Libya Detailed', *Washington Post*, 23 March 1990.

41. Ibid.

42. See, e.g., James Adams, *Engines of War* (Cambridge, MA: Atlantic Monthly Press, 1990), *passim*; 'Belgian Police Report Uncovering Arms Ring', *New York Times*, 9 Nov. 1986; Michael T. Klare, 'The Secret Sources of Terrorists' Weapons', *Long Island Newsday*, 8 Sept. 1987; Michael T. Klare, 'Secret operatives, clandestine trades: the thriving black market for weapons', *Bulletin of the Atomic Scientists*, April 1988, pp.16–24; John W. Soule, 'Problems in Applying Counterterrorism to Prevent Terrorism: Two Decades of Violence in Northern Ireland Reconsidered', *Terrorism* (Jan./Feb. 1989), p.38; Ronald J. Ostrow, '2 Colombians Arrested in Plot to Buy Missiles', *Los Angeles Times*, 8 May 1990; Leonard Doyle, 'Irishmen convicted of plot to buy missile', *Independent* (London), 12 Dec. 1990; David McKittrick, 'Arms for Africa fuel paramilitary terror', *Independent* (London), 29 Oct. 1991; and 'Guns: Buyer's Market', *The Economist*, 16 May 1992.

43. Herrhausen, for example, travelled in an armour-plated limousine often accompanied by two additional carloads of bodyguards in addition to those riding with him; checked luggage on Pan Am flights was supposedly subject to x-ray (which would not, in any event, have detected the Semtex plastic explosive) and tracked by a sophisticated computer luggage-accountability system.

44. A similar, unexploded device has been discovered on board a Pan Am flight departing from Rio de Janiero Airport four years before. For details of both devices, see Billie H. Vincent, 'Statement by Mr Billie H. Vincent Before a Subcommittee of the Committee on Government Operations, House of Representatives', 25/26 Sept. 1989.

45. Ibid.

46. David Rose, 'Devices reveal IRA know-how', *Guardian* (London), 18 May 1990.

47. Michael Smith, 'IRA Use of Radar Guns in Bombings Described', *Daily Telegraph* (London), 20 May 1991.

48. Ibid. See also, David Hearts, 'IRA mines gap in army security', *Guardian* (London), 10 April, 1990; David Hearts, '"Human bomb" fails to explode', *Guardian* (London), 24 Nov. 1990; Jamie Dettmer and Edward Gorman, 'Seven dead in IRA "human" bomb attacks', *The Times* (London), 25 Oct. 1990; Will Bennet, 'Terrorists keep changing tactics to elude security forces', *Independent* (London), 17 Dec. 1991.

49. Ibid.

50. Quoted in 'Outrage not a reason for inaction', *Manchester Guardian International Edition* 21 Oct. 1984.

51. Stewart Tendler, 'A crude and lethal weapon to thwart the security forces', *The Times* (London), 8 Feb. 1991; and Will Bennet, 'Simple bombs improved but lack accuracy', *Independent* (London), 8 Feb. 1991.

52. As one high-ranking PIRA terrorist explained, 'You change your tactics to keep them guessing. It all depends on logistics. If you stick to one tactic, you can become

predictable and be tracked down. They can find out when you work to a pattern.'
Quoted in Will Bennett, 'Terrorists keep changing tactics to elude security forces',
Independent (London), 17 Dec. 1991.

53. Margaret L. Rogg, 'Sudanese Airliner With 60 On Board Downed By Missile', *New
York Times*, 18 Aug. 1986; and Patrick Brogan, *The Fighting Never Stopped: A Guide
to World Conflict Since 1945* (NY: Vintage Books, 1990), p.xiii. UNITA (the
National Union for Total Independence of Angola) claims to have shot down at least
three civilian aircraft. In 1985 the Afghani government reported that mujahedin shot
down a civilian airliner killing its 52 passengers. See David Isby, 'Sons of SAM',
Soldier of Fortune, March 1989, pp.30–1.

54. James Adams and David Leppard, 'IRA set to use SAM-7 missiles in terror drive,'
Sunday Times (London), 19 Feb. 1989.

55. Howell Raines, 'Machine Guns Due on Ulster Copters', *New York Times*, 7 Jan.
1988.

56. See David Isby, 'Sons of SAM', pp.30–1; Robert Fox, 'Arms sales ready to rocket',
Daily Telegraph (London), 6 March, 1990; and Michael R. Gordon, 'CIA. Sees a Developing World With Developed Arms', *New York Times*, 10 Feb. 1989. Indeed,
agents acting on behalf of the PIRA and the Medellin cocaine cartel have attempted
to obtain US-made Stinger surface-to-air missiles. See Emile Lounsberry and David
Pallister, 'IRA rocket launcher seized,' *Guardian* (London), 15 July 1989; Business
Risks International *Risk Assessment Weekly* 6/33, 18 Aug. 1989; 'Irish face weapons
charges in US' *Guardian* (London), 15 Jan. 1990; Business Risks International, *Risk
Assessment Weekly* 7/3, 19 Jan. 1990; Michael Isikoff, 'Two Colombians Arrested In
Scheme to Buy Missiles', *Washington Post*, 8 May 1990; and Jeff Garth, 'FBI Said to
Foil Missile Smuggling to Colombia', *New York Times*, 7 May 1990.

57. US officials are already concerned that Stinger missiles provided to Afghani mujahedin for use in their struggle against Soviet occupying forces are now either appearing
on the black market or being sold to Islamic radicals in other countries. See Steve
LeVine, 'US now worries terrorists may get Stinger', *Washington Times*, 31 Dec.
1991; Robert S. Greenberger, 'Afghan Guerrilla Leader Armed by US Hekmatyar,
Could Prove Embarrassing', *Wall Street Journal*, 11 May 1992; and Richard S. Ehr-
lich, 'For Sale in Afghanistan: US-supplied Stingers', *Washington Times*, 21 May
1991.

58. Brian M. Jenkins, *The Likelihood of Nuclear Terrorism* (Santa Monica, CA: RAND
Corp., P-7119, July 1986), p.6.

59. Thesis originally advanced by the author in collaboration with Peter deLeon in *The
Threat of Nuclear Terrorism: A Reexamination* (Santa Monica, CA:RAND, N-2706,
Jan. 1988).

60. Followed by Israel, France, Great Britain, West Germany, the Soviet Union,
Turkey, Cuba, Spain, and Iran. Source: The RAND Chronology of International
Terrorism.

61. One can envisage ethnic, nationalist, and irredentist minorities turning to the US for
support and intervention, which, if not provided, could act as a catalyst for increased
anti-American terrorism designed to coerce the United States to intervene on their
behalf or to punish the United States for not intervening. Of course, terrorism designed to protest or reverse US intervention in local conflicts (such as was the case in
Lebanon during the 1980s) is likely to continue as well.

Non-Traditional Explosives: Potential Detection Problems

JIMMIE C. OXLEY

Most explosive detection technologies have been focused on nitro-based military explosives because, indeed, they have figured in international terrorist incidents Not only are they readily available through purchase or theft or from sponsoring states, but methods for home synthesis of TNT, PETN and RDX are widely available. Presently substantial resources are being committed to developing explosive detection technologies to protect commercial aircraft, trains, tunnels, nuclear powerplants, etc. against such terrorist threats. Most of the systems now under development target a specific characteristic of military or commercial explosives (e.g., mass density, nitrogen density). However, as counter-terrorist measures make traditional explosives more difficult to obtain or more risky to use, we should anticipate terrorists may turn to non-traditional explosives. There are hundreds of energetic compounds and many common explosives which, while they do not meet exacting military demands, would be effective terrorist tools.

Although explosive handbooks list hundreds of explosives, the following discussion focuses on only a handful. These have been chosen because they meet the following criteria.

They are explosives or pyrotechnics that do not follow the classic patterns of military explosives, which new detection technologies are expected to target.

The selected energetic compounds are easily obtainable or are readily prepared.

This paper will also point out energetic systems that can produce violently exothermic reactions without the aid of traditional initiating systems, such as batteries or detonators.

Terrorist attacks generally fall into three broad categories: assassination; seizure (e.g., highjacking); and explosive destruction of a major asset, usually accompanied by substantial loss of life. The 1990s Mafia-linked assassinations in Sicily indicate the difficulties of protecting more-or-less private individuals against well-equipped and determined terrorists; this is unlikely to change in the foreseeable future. Seizures or highjackings of embassies, commercial aircraft, cruise ships, etc. have and should continue to decline if existing and emerging counter-measures are implemented in conjunction with sound physical security practices. (In fact, the increase in attempts to destroy commercial aircraft during the past few years may be due to the improvements in anti-seizure technologies and practices.)

Explosive destruction can be accomplished externally or internally. Examples of external attacks include the use of shoulder fired surface-to-air missiles or mines laid on or under railroad tracks. This threat will not be addressed. Examples of internal attacks include all manner of improvised explosive devices smuggled onto commercial aircraft, into government buildings, etc. This paper will focus on technological developments in the area of internal explosive destruction. This is the area in which the greatest research and development efforts have been focused in recent years. The US Federal Aviation Administration, a world leader in this area, has spent well over $100 million on explosive detection R&D during the past decade, and the pace has been increasing. Furthermore, this is the area in which terrorists may have the greatest opportunities for circumventing the emerging counter-terrorist technologies.

Background

An explosion is a rapid expansion of matter into much greater volume. The expansion is such that the energy is transferred almost completely into mass motion, and this is accompanied by loud noise and a great deal of heat. Explosive devices may be mechanical, chemical, or atomic. An explosive substance is one which reacts chemically to produce heat and gas and a rapid expansion of matter. A detonation is a very special type of explosion. It is a rapid chemical reaction, initiated by the heat accompanying a shock compression, which liberates sufficient energy, before any expansion occurs, to sustain the shock wave. The shock wave propagates into the unreacted material at supersonic speed, between 1500 and 900 m/s.

Typical military explosives are organic chemicals; usually they contain only four types of atoms: carbon (C), hydrogen (H), oxygen (O), and nitrogen (N). To achieve maximum volume change, gas information, and heat release, explosives are designed to be dense, to have high oxygen content, and to have positive heats of formation. In monomolecular, organic explosives, this means explosives usually contain NO_2 groups. Upon detonation, exothermic reactions occur which transform nitrogen atoms into nitrogen (N_2) gas, while the oxygen atoms combine with the hydrogen and carbon atoms to form the gaseous products H_2O, CO, or CO_2. This is similar to what happens in combustion, but a detonation is different from burning in two ways. In combustion, there is an unlimited amount of oxidiser available. An explosive reacts so quickly that it must have its own source of oxygen near at hand, either in the same molecule, as with most military explosives (e.g., TNT), or in a neighbouring molecule, as in the intimate mixture of ammonium nitrate and fuel oil (ANFO).

$$4\ C_7H_5N_3O_6\ (TNT) \rightarrow 7\ CO_2 + 6\ N_2 + 10\ H_2O + 21\ C$$
$$37\ NH_4NO_3 + CH_3(CH_2)_{10}CH_3 \rightarrow 12\ CO_2 + 37\ N_2 + 87\ H_2O$$

'Oxygen Balance' is a method of quantifying how well an explosive provides its own oxidant. There are various ways of defining oxygen balance (OB). One can balance the oxygen so that every carbon has one oxygen (balanced for CO) or so that every carbon has two oxygen (balanced for CO_2).[1] One can also balance in terms of weight percent oxygen in the explosive (OB) or in terms of oxidant per 100 grams explosive (OB_{100}).[2]

The second way in which a detonation differs from a fast burn (deflagration) is the manner in which the performance is evaluated. The performance of a fuel is based on the amount of heat it releases; the performance of an explosive has some relation to the heat it releases, but there is more involved than that. Detonation is unique in the rapid rate at which energy is released. A high explosive creates a tremendous power density:

	W/cm^3
Burning acetylene	10^2
Deflagrating propellant	10^6
Detonating high explosive	10^{10}

The performance of an explosive cannot be expressed in a single characteristic. Performance is dependent on the detonation rate or velocity, the packing density, the gas liberated per unit weight, and the heat of explosion. Detonation velocity, itself, is dependent on packing density, charge diameter, degree of confinement, and particle size.

Both the terms brisance and strength are used in describing the performance of an explosive. When an explosive detonates there is a practically instantaneous pressure jump from the shock wave. The subsequent expansion of the detonation gases performs work, moves objects, but it is the pressure jump which shatters or fragments objects. Brisance (from French for shatter) is a description of the destructive fragmentation effect on a charge upon its immediate vicinity. Since shattering effect is dependent upon the suddenness of the pressure rise, it is most dependent upon detonation velocity. Brisance is the term of importance in military applications. Brisance is often evaluated from detonation velocity, but there are 'crusher' tests in which the compression of lead or copper blocks by the detonation of the test explosive is taken as a measure of brisance.[1] Strength is important in mining operations; it describes how much rock can be moved. The strength of an explosive is more related to the total gas yield and the heat of explosion. It is often quantified with the Trauzl lead block test, where ten grams of a test sample are placed in a $61cm^3$ hole in a lead block and initiated with a No.8 blasting cap. Performance is evaluated from the size of the cavity created in the lead block.[3]

Explosives are often classified by the stimuli to which they respond and the degree of response. Propellants or deflagrating or low explosives are combustible materials containing within themselves all oxygen needful for their combustion. Examples are black powder and smokeless powder (colloided nitrocellulose). Detonating or 'high' explosives are characterised by their high rate of reaction and high pressure. In TNT or nitroglycerin, both high explosives, the shock wave travels at a speed of 6000 m/sec, compared to gun powder, a low explosive, in which it travels at 100 m/s.

High explosives are subdivided into primary and secondary by the way they are initiated into the detonation, primary explosives are detonated by simple ignition-spark, flame, impact. They do not burn nor even necessarily contain the elements needed to burn. An explosion results whether they are confined or not. Examples of primary explosives are lead azide, lead picrate, lead styphnate, mercury fulminate, m-nitrophenyldiazonium perchlorate, tetracene, nitrogen sulphide (N_4S_4), copper acetylide, fulminating gold, nitrosoguanidine, potassium chlorate with red phosphorus (P_4), and the tartarate and oxalate salts of mercury and silver.

Secondary explosives require a detonator or primary explosive. Secondary explosives differ from primary explosives in not being initiated readily by impact or electrostatic discharge, and they do not easily undergo a deflagration-to-detonation transition (DDT). They can be initiated by large shocks; usually they are initiated by the shock created by a primary explosive. A fuze or blasting cap and frequently a booster are required. (A booster is a sensitive secondary explosive which reinforces the detonation wave from the detonator into the main charge). Like primary explosives, secondary explosives do not burn, nor do they require confinement. In general, they are more powerful, brisant, than primary explosives. Examples of secondary explosives include nitrocellulose, nitroglycerin, dynamite, TNT, picric acid, tetryl,

RDX, HMX, nitroguanidine, ammonium nitrate, ammonium perchlorate, liquid oxygen mixed with wood pulp, fuming nitric acid mixed with nitrobenzene, compressed acetylene and cyanogen.

Military explosives are secondary explosives, and they usually fall into one of three categories all of which contain nitro NO_2 groups. Nitrate esters, for example, nitroglycerin, nitrocellulose, PETN (active component in DETA sheet), contain $O-NO_2$ groups. These are possibly by oldest explosives still used by the military, nitration of alcohols having become a popular research topic in the 1830s and 1840s. Nitroglycerin and nitrocellulose became useful explosives by the 1860s. Nitrate esters are also the least stable military explosives; they lose NO_2 readily, making them relatively easy targets for vapour detection. Nitroarenes with a $C-NO_2$ linkage are typified by TNT (component of Composition B) or picric acid. Nitramines contain $N-NO_2$ groups; typical examples RDX and HMX are often the active components in plastic-bonded explosives such as Composition B, C-4, and Semtex.[4,5]

nitrate ester	nitroarenes		nitramine

$$O_2NOCH_2-\underset{\underset{CH_2ONO_2}{|}}{\overset{\overset{CH_2ONO_2}{|}}{C}}-CH_2NO_2$$

nitroarenes: TNT structure (CH_3 top, O_2NC, CNO_2, HC, CH, C, NO_2)

picric acid structure (OH top, O_2NC, CNO_2, HC, CH, C, NO_2)

RDX structure (O_2NN, NNO_2, CH_2, H_2C, CH_2, N, NO_2)

	PETN	TNT	picric acid	RDX
Discovery	1894	1863	1742	1899
Used	1930	1900	1870	1940
g/cm^3	1.67	1.64	1.70	1.77
m/s	7975	6942	7480	8639
Cal/g	1510	1090	1270	1510

Discussion

Present explosive detection technology has focused on military explosives; and, indeed, they have figured in international terrorist incidents. Not only are they readily available for purchase or theft, but methods for home synthesis of TNT,[6] picric acid,[6,7,8] lead picrate,[7,8] PETN[9,10] and RDX[9] are widely available. However, there are hundreds of energetic compounds and many common explosives which, while they do not meet exacting military demands, would be effective terrorist tools. Therefore, as present day interdiction technology becomes more familiar to the public, we should anticipate terrorists may turn to non-military explosives.

Although explosive handbooks[1,3] list hundreds of explosives, the following discussion focuses on only a handful. These have been chosen because they meet at two of the following criteria. They must be explosives or pyrotechnics which do not follow the classic patterns of military explosives, which new detection technologies are expected to target. The selected energetic compounds are easily obtainable or are readily prepared. There is an attempt to point out energetic systems which can produce a violently exothermic reaction without the aid of a traditional initiating system.

Possible non-nitro-explosives can be identified by consulting the propellant, pyrotechnic, and fuel/air explosive literature. Many of these energetic materials can be classed as composite explosives, intimate mixtures of fuels and oxidisers. Peroxides are unique in that they can function as oxidisers in composite explosives or as stand-alone explosives, and triacetone triperoxide has reportedly been used in several terrorist incidents. Several self-igniting systems such as boranes, phosphorus, and alkali metals are discussed; for many of these, a blasting cap is not a requirement. In addition to non-nitrogen-containing energetic materials, several nitrogen-containing explosives in which nitrogen is not a part of the conventional nitro-group, will be discussed; included in this class is ammonium nitrate, the most available explosive worldwide.

Civilian Nitrogen-Containing Explosives

Nitromethane CH_3NO_2 is one of the few nitroalkanes which finds occasional applications as an explosive. It is a common industrial solvent and has a unique use as a fuel additive in hobby rockets and race cars. The explosive properties of nitromethane have been extensively studied since it is a relatively simple explosive (heat of explosion 1063cal/g; detonation velocity 6290m/s at density 1.138g/cm^3; lead block test 400cm^3). Although various propellant and explosive compositions have been patented, and for a time its use as a liquid monopropellant was considered, nitromethane has found no widespread military use. As a blasting agent, gelled nitromethane (gelled with guar gum or nitrocellulose) is comparable to ANFO (ammonium nitrate/fuel oil); it is more difficult to handle, but its higher density produces a high detonation velocity and energy output.[1]

The physical properties of nitromethane are such, a clear liquid with boiling point 101°C, melting point −17°C, and density 1.14g/cc (at 15°C),[4] that it could easily pass as water except for its unique odour (vapour pressure 37mm at 25°C). However, if nitromethane or a formulation

containing it, such as PLX, were bottled, with present detection technology, it would be very difficult to distinguish from water or wine. PLX
(Picatinny Liquid Explosive), a slightly yellow liquid, contains 95 per
cent nitromethane and 5 per cent ethylenediamine.[1] It was developed
during World War II for mine-clearing operations. It was intended that
the two ingredients be mixed just prior to use. PLX, in a whisky bottle,
and 350g of Composition C4 in a radio were reportedly used in the
downing of Korean Air Flight 858 (November 1987).

Ammonium Nitrate (AN, NH_4NO_3) is perhaps the most important
raw material in the manufacture of industrial explosives (heat of explosion 627cal/g; detonation velocity 1000–3000m/s; lead block test
180cm^3). In 1986 over 11 billion pounds of ammonium nitrate were produced in the USA. Although its end use is mainly fertilizer, almost 20
per cent of it finds use in the explosive industry.[11],[12] Ammonium nitrate
has been used in explosive applications since 1867 when two Swedish
chemists patented an explosive which used AN alone or mixed with
charcoal, sawdust, napththalene, picric acid, nitroglycerin, or nitrobenzene. Nobel purchased the invention and used AN in dynamites.
Amatol, developed during World War I, was a mixture of AN and TNT
in various proportions: 50/50, 60/40, or 80/20. Amatols are not as brisant
as TNT; the more AN, the less brisant and the lower the detonation
velocity.[13]

Pure ammonium nitrate is considered an oxidiser rather than an explosive. AN was not considered an explosive until the 1921 disaster in
Oppau, Germany, killing almost 600 people. In 1947 two different incidents occurred with ships loaded with fertilizer grade (wax-coated)
ammonium nitrate (FEAN). In the first event at Texas City, Texas, the
detonation of two shiploads of AN took about 600 lives; in the second in
Brest, France, 20 died. When combustible non-explosives are added to
ammonium nitrate, they react with the excess oxygen in AN to produce
additional gas and heat, increasing the power and temperature of the explosion. The combustible non-explosive can be rosin, sulphur, charcoal,
flour, sugar, oil, or paraffin, but most often it is a fuel oil. ANFO is a
mixture of ammonium nitrate with 5–6 per cent fuel oil.

$$37 \ NH_4NO_3 \ + \ CH_3(CH_2)_{10}CH_3 \rightarrow 12 \ CO_2 + 37 \ N_2 + 87 \ H_2O$$

The preparation of ANFO can be as simple as pouring a fuel over a bag
of ammonium nitrate. AN may be mixed more intimately with fuel in
gels or emulsions. These materials came into use in the mining industry
in the 1950s and 1960s, almost completely replacing dynamite. A typical
ammonium nitrate aqueous emulsion contains 80 per cent AN, 14 per
cent water, and 6 per cent fuel mixed with an emulsifier. Such a mixture
can be easily whipped up in any kitchen.

The availability of ammonium nitrate is such that do-it-at-home explosives books[6],[8] list many explosive formulations derived from it, and another such publication[14] labels ANFO as 'homemade C-4' and gives detailed instructions as to the proper grade of AN to purchase. Even AN mixed with aluminium is reported to be a powerful explosive.[8]

Ammonium Perchlorate is made by the electrochemical oxidation of sodium chloride NaCl to the chlorate $NaClO_3$ and on to the perchlorate $NaClO_4$. Like ammonium nitrate, ammonium perchlorate (of particle size greater than 45um) has been classed as an oxidizer rather than as an explosive for purposes of shipping (heat of explosion 4488cal/g; detonation velocity 3400m/s; lead block test 195cm^3). If the Texas City disaster of 1947 emphasised the explosive capacity of AN, then the PEPCON detonation of 1988, where half the US AP production capacity was lost and two people were killed, demonstrated the explosive power of AP. Both the French and Germans used ammonium perchlorate explosives during World War I.[13] The TNT equivalence of AP is about 0.31.

Mercury Fulminate $Hg(ONC)_2$ is a primary explosive, sensitive to heat, friction, and light (heat of explosion 355cal/g, detonation velocity 3500m/s at density 2g/cm^3). It undergoes marked decomposition above 50°C and is usually stored under water. Until the development of lead azide, mercury fulminate was practically the only explosive used in primers, basting caps and detonators, either by itself or in composition. Now it has largely been replaced by lead azide or diazodinitrophenol. Used in combination with fuels such as antimony sulphide (Sb_2S_3), mercury fulminate merely deflagrates, but in the presence of $KClO_c$, it can be used to ignite propellants. The synthesis of mercury fulminate is that the synthesis is included in several do-it-at-home explosives books.[6],[8],[10] Mercury is dissolved in concentrated nitric acid, ethanol is added, and the white crystals of mercury fulminate formed are thoroughly washed.

Azides are roughly divided into three classes: stable ionic azides (alkali and alkaline earth azides); unstable covalent azides (haloazides) which frequently explode spontaneously; and heavy-metal azides [$Pb(N_3)_2$, AgN_3] that explode with shock. It is the latter group which is often used as primers for initiating high explosives. The usual synthetic route is reaction of the metal nitrate with sodium azide.[15]

$$Pb(NO_3)_2 + 2\ NaN_3 \rightarrow Pb(N_3)_2 + 2\ NaNO_3$$

The synthesis of sodium azide has been published so that the terrorist can prepare it and, hence, lead azide, in his kitchen.[7] However, sodium azide itself will soon be widely available as it is used in most automobile air bags; and in many passenger-side air bags up to a half pound is used. Lead azide has respectable explosive properties (heat of explosion 367cal/g; detonation velocity 5300m/s at density 4.6g/cm^3; lead block test 110cm^3).

Nitrogen Triiodide NI$_3$, due to its low brisance and high sensitivity, has no practical use in the energetic materials community.[1] However, it has remained a favourite of teenagers due to its ready synthesis. This is probably the reason its synthesis is also included in the do-it-at-home explosive literature.[6] Iodine crystals are added slowly to concentrated ammonium hydroxide. A brownish-red precipitate forms. The precipitate is filtered and washed with alcohol and ether. This material can be handled only when wet because when dry, the slightest touch, such as a fly, can set it off.

Urea Nitrate Urea nitrate is stable, does not deliquesce, and is a powerful, cool explosive (heat of explosion 796gal/g; detonation velocity 3400m/s at density 0.86g/cm^3; lead block test 270cm^3). Its disadvantage for military use is that it is corrosively acidic in the presence of moisture.

$$(NH_2)_2 - C = O + HNO_3 \rightarrow (NH_2)_2 - C = O \cdot HNO_3$$

Although this material may be easily detectable, it is included in this listing of terrorist opportunities because it is often cited in the do-it-at-home literature and because the cited starting materials nitric acid and urine are easily obtained.[8] This is probably a good illustration that nitration, practiced on a variety of materials, yields an explosive–sugar, cotton clothing, aluminium foil.

Urea nitrate can be made more powerful by adding aluminium or by drastic dehydration.[7,8] Nitrourea, prepared by dehydration of urea nitrate with concentrated sulphuric acid, is a much more powerful explosive, a nitramine, in fact (heat of explosion 923cal/g).[16] Nitrourea decomposes in the presence of moisture.

Nitrogen-Free Explosives

Some potential non-nitrogenous explosives can be identified by consulting the propellant, pyrotechnic, and fuel/air-explosive literature. The boundary between such energetic mixtures is often vague, since the terms propellant, pyrotechnic, and explosive tend to be used to describe end uses rather than chemical composition. A propellant and an explosive can have the same active ingredient. Most of potential non-nitrogenous explosives can be broadly classed as composite explosives. Rather than containing the oxidiser and fuel in a single molecule, as do the organic military explosives, composite explosives are formed by intimately mixing oxidising compound(s) with fuel(s). These can be pre-mixed or mixed just prior to use. In such mixtures there can be problems due to inhomogeneities; the finer the solid particle size and the more intimate the mix, the better the performance.

A classic example of a composite explosive is black powder, a mixture of the oxidizers KNO_3 and sulphur with the fuel charcoal. As with black powder, the performance of many of these mixtures is related to the degree of confinement. ANFO, a mixture of ammonium nitrate and fuel oil, is another good example of a composite explosive. While military explosives have been common in international terrorism, in domestic terrorism in the US black powder, smokeless powder (nitrocellulose based) and flash powder (KNO_3, $KClO_4$, sulphur) have been the three most common explosive fillers.[17]

Tables 1 and 2 below list oxidisers and fuels which can be combined to form composite explosives. Most contain no nitrogen and are either commercially available or easily prepared.[18]

TABLE 1

OXIDISERS

oxygen and halogens	
perchlorates	$KClO_4$ & NH_4, Na, Ba, Ca salts
chlorates	$KClO_3$ & Li, Na, Ba salts
hypochlorite	$Ca(OCl)_2$
nitrates	KNO_3 & NH_4, Na, Ba, Ag, Sr salts
chromates	$PbCrO_4$ & Ba, Ca, K salts
dichromates	$K_2Cr_2O_7$ & $NH_4Cr_2O_7$
iodates	KIO_3 & Pb, Ag salts
permanganate	$KMnO_4$
metal oxides	BaO_2, Cu_2O, CuO, Fe_2O_3, Fe_3O_4, PbO_2, Pb_3O_4, PbO, MnO_2, ZnO
peroxides	Na_2O_2, H_2O_2 (80%), dibenzoylperoxide

TABLE 2

FUELS

nitrobenzene	petroleum	halogenated hydrocarbons
nitrotuoluenes	turpentine	halogens
nitronaphthalene	naphtha	powdered metals
nitrocellulose	castor oil	carbon disulphide (CS_2)
picric acid	sugar	phosphorus (P_4)
	glycerin	sulphur (S_8)
	acetylene	
	wax, paraffin	
	sawdust	

Liquid Oxidisers In 1895 liquid oxygen explosives (LOX) were invented by Linde, who had developed a successful machine for the liquefaction of gases. LOX are formed by impregnating porous combustible materials with liquid oxygen. Lampblack is the absorbent combustible most commonly used. The detonation velocity of the C/O_2 mixture averages 3000m/s.[19] Two problems exist with liquid oxygen containing explosives: they lose their explosiveness as the liquid oxygen evaporates (boiling point $-183°C$); and they are easily inflamed. During World War I the Germans use LOX when other explosives ran low. In 1926 LOX were used for the first time in commercial rock blasting operations; their use was continued into the 1960s.

Acetylene is usually thought of as a highly flammable gas, but it is also detonable as a gas, as a liquid (boiling point $-80°C$), or as a solid (melting/freezing point $-84°C$), acetylene is an explosive. The detonation velocity of solid acetylene is 2270m/s; combined with liquid oxygen (acetylene 25% /O_2 75%) the detonation velocity is comparable to high explosives (6000m/s).[1]

$$H-C≡C-H + liq\ O_2 → 2\ CO_2 + H_2O$$

Below 21°C nitrogen dioxide (NO_2), a toxic gas, condenses to a colourless liquid, nitrogen tetroxide (N_2O_4). Below $-11°C$ it becomes solid.

$$2\ NO_2\ (g) ⟷ am\ N_2O_4\ (liq)$$

Explosives made with liquid N_2O_4 and combustible liquids (carbon disulphide, nitrbenzene, nitrotoluene, gasoline, halogenated hydrocarbons) were first suggested in 1881 and were generally termed Panclastities. The Germans tested marine torpedoes containing sealed glass container of N_2O_4 and CS_2 in the 1880s; set-back forces broke the glass containers generating the explosive mixture, and an impact fuze initiated detonation. In World War I, when other explosives were in short supply, the French used Anilites, where liquid N_2O_4 and a fuel were enclosed in separated compartments of a bomb; after the bomb was dropped, passage of air by the nose opened a valve permitting the two liquids to mix.[13] In World War II Panclastites were used in some of the heaviest British aircraft bombs.

Panclastites are inexpensive and easy to prepare; some are more brisant and have better detonation velocities than TNT or picric acid. However, though their performance is favourable, Panclastites are too shock sensitive, too hard to handle, to find common military use. Their extreme sensitivity dictates that they be mixed just prior to use, and the corrosive nature of N_2O_4 requires special vessels. The N_2O_4/fuel mixtures can be absorbed on Kieselguhr to form a soft non-plastic material, which has too high a freezing point for military use. A mixture of 35 parts of carbon disulphide/NB (35/65) with 65 parts N_2O_4 has a lead block test of 435cm^3. Mixtures of N_2O_4 with 64 per cent nitromethane have a detonation velocity of 6900m/s. Nitrogen tetroxide explodes on contact with several fuels: acetic anhydride, liquid ammonia, methyl and ethyl nitrate, propene, hydrazine-type fuels.

Oxides of Chlorine Among the oxides of chlorine, perchlorate is the most stable, but all are energetic and produce toxic fumes. Only chloric and perchloric acids can be isolated. Their reactivity follows that of the salts. They violently react with combustible, chloric acid being the more reactive.

$$ClO^- < ClO_2^- < ClO_3^- < ClO_4^-$$
hypochlorite chlorite chlorate perchlorate

In World War II the US used Galcit propellant that incorporated $KClO_4$ (75 per cent) into molten asphalt (25 per cent).[1,3] It was the precursor of modern composite propellants in which ammonium perchlorate is embedded in a polymer. $KClO_4$, mixed with MnO_2 and a fuel, ignites spontaneously.

Among the oxidizers, chlorates ClO_3^-, are especially hazardous to handle. They decompose exothermically and are sensitive to heat, impact, and friction. Many chlorate mixtures, particularly those which contain sulphur, sulphide, or picric acid are extremely sensitive to blows and friction. The sensitivity can be reduced by phlegmatization in castor oil. Chlorate explosives with aromatic nitro compounds have higher detonation velocities and are more brisant than those in which the carbonaceous material is merely combustible. In 1885, 240,000lb of a mixture of $KClO_3$ (70 per cent) and nitrobenzene (21 per cent) along with 42,000lb dynamite were used to blast a portion of Hell Gate Channel in New York harbour. Other similar mixtures are turpentine/phenol (90/10) absorbed on $KClO_3/MnO_2$ (80/20) or nitrobenzene/turpentine (80/20) absorbed on $KClO_3/KMnO_4$ (70/30).

Mixtures of chlorate and fuel will spontaneously ignite with the addition of a drop of concentrated sulphuric acid (H_2SO_4). Spontaneous ignition or explosion can occur when alkali chlorates are combined with very reactive fuels (such as phosphorus, sulphur, powdered arsenic, or selenium) or with moist fuels. In fact, when powdered, dry, unoxidized $KClO_3$ and red phosphorus (Armstrong's powder) are pushed together, they ignite; this reaction has been tamed and utilised by use of separation and a binder in the common safety match. Armstrong's powder, wet with some volatile solvent such as methanol, has been used as an antipersonnel device. MnO_2 has been reported as a catalyst for the decomposition of chlorates. One do-it-at-home explosive book suggests an explosive filler of 9 parts $KClO_3$ and 1 part petroleum jelly or 3 parts $NaClO_3$ to 2 part aluminium or 3 parts $NaClO_3$ to 2 parts sugar.[8]

Calcium hypochlorite [$Ca(OCl)_2$] ignites spontaneously with glycerin.

Hypochlorites are generally highly reactive and unstable, but the calcium salt (HTH) is one of the more stable hypochlorites with the abbreviation HTH. Many forms of hypochlorite are available to the public: as liquid household bleach (an alkaline solution of NaOCl); as household dish washing detergents and scouring powders $[(Na_3PO_{411}H_2O)_4 NaOCl]$; as a liquid bleach for pulp and paper bleaching [a mixture of $Ca(OCl)_2$ and $CaCl_2$]; and as a powdered swimming pool bleach $[Ca(OCl)_2/CaCl_2/Ca(OH)_2 2H_2O]$. Discussing a mixture of 70 per cent HTH (from a swimming pool supply house) and petroleum naphtha (sold in hardware and paint stores) in a 30/1 ratio, one do-it-at-home book states, 'This mixture forms a low power/brisant high explosive which should be used under strong confinement and only as an explosive filler for antipersonnel fragmentation bombs.'[8]

Metals Some alkali metals spontaneously ignite on exposure to water or air. As the alkali metals increase in weight, their reaction to air becomes more violent. While potassium may oxidise so rapidly that it melts and ignites when pressure is applied (as in cutting), cesium burns in air as soon as it is removed from an inert oil covering. Moisture in the air serves to enhance further reactivity. Sodium and potassium form a eutectic (NaK) which is spontaneously ignitable. Sodium/potassium alloys are reported to react explosively upon contact with silver halides or to detonate upon contact with halogenated organic materials such as carbon tetrachloride. Potassium and heavier alkali metals burst into flame upon contact with water. Sodium too will inflame in water if it can be anchored in one spot long enough to allow the heat of reaction to ignite the hydrogen being produced:

$$Na + H_2O \rightarrow NaOH + 1/2 H_2.$$

Lithium is the least reactive alkali metal but will ignite if thrown on water as a dispersion. In World War II the Germans used land mines composed of sodium and methyl nitrate in separate compartments. Pressure brought the two together and into action.

Some finely-divided (powdered) non-alkali metals will also burst into flame in the presence of air. The best known are lead, iron, nickel, cobalt, and aluminium. These can be prepared by pyrolysis of their organic salts or by reduction of their oxides, or in some cases, by formation of a mercury amalgam. These metals may also explosively react with water, halogenated hydrocarbons, and halogens. One do-it-at-home explosives book suggests the syrupy mixture of powdered aluminium and carbon tetrachloride as a cap sensitive explosive; the source of aluminium is the paint store.[8]

$$Al + CCl_4 \rightarrow AlCl_3$$

Magnesium is used in several pyrotechnics. When a magnesium/silver nitrate mixture is moistened, it reacts explosively. Teflon $(C_2F_4)_n$ with powdered magnesium reacts explosively upon ignition. Devices of this composition are used as decoys for heat-seeking missiles.

$$(C_2F_4)_n + 2n \text{ Mg} \rightarrow 2n \text{ C} + 2n \text{ MgF}_2$$

Some methyl- and ethyl-substituted metals are spontaneously ignitable in air. The alkylated metals most frequently exhibiting this behaviour are the alkali metals (Li, Na), aluminium, zinc, and arsenic or non-metals such as boron and phosphorus. Many of these compounds also react explosively with water and with carbon tetrachloride, (CCl_4). It is reported that triethylaluminum $[Al(C_2H_5)_3]$ in carbon tetrachloride reacts explosively when warmed to room temperature.

Thermite is generally the redox reaction between a metal oxide and a metal. However, the most important reaction and the one usually referred to by this name is that of aluminium and iron oxide:

$$8 \text{ Al} + 3 \text{ Fe}_3O_4 \rightarrow 4 \text{ Al}_2O_3 + 9 \text{ Fe}$$

This reaction generates a tremendous amount of heat; molten iron is produced and its melting point is above 1530°C. One peaceful application of this reaction is for welding in shipyards and railroads. In fact one home-military manual[8] cites these as likely places to obtain pre-mixed thermite for incendiary devices. With $KMnO_4$ in the metal mixture, reaction can be triggered with added glycerol. With sugar in the initial mix, reaction is triggered with a drop of concentrated H_2SO_4. Thermite reactions using CuO or Mn_3O_4 are reported explosive. Mixtures of Pb, PbO_2, and PbO also undergo explosive thermite reactions.

Acetylides Some metal carbides exist which are explosive in their own right; most are termed acetylides rather than carbides. Copper acetylide and silver acetylide are most commonly prepared by teenagers. Being primary explosives, they explode violently upon heating, impact, or friction. Cuprous acetylide is the only acetylide which has been used in the explosives industry; it has been used in electric detonators. Acetylides can be formed by passing acetylene through a solution of the appropriate metal salt.

Peroxides Peroxides, with oxygen in the -1 oxidation state, can be violent oxidizers in the presence of fuel. For example, sodium peroxide Na_2O_2 instantly ignites in the presence of moisture and a fuel (magnesium and sawdust or paper, or sulphur or aluminium). In addition to this feature, peroxides also can undergo a violent self-decomposition. Peroxide decomposition into water and oxygen can be catalysed by small amount of alkaline lead, silver or manganese salts or even saliva.[1,20]

Hydrogen peroxide may be a particularly appealing alternative to traditional explosives since bottled it can easily pass as mineral water. Pure hydrogen peroxide decomposes violently above 80°C; therefore, it is sold as aqueous solutions (27.5, 35, 50, and 70 per cent in water). It is available at local pharmacies as a 3 per cent solution for use as disinfectant or as a 40 per cent solution for use as a hair lightener or as a gel to brighten teeth. It can also be concentrated in the laboratory. Pure hydrogen peroxide is readily detonable with a heat of explosion of 24.6kcal/mol. Hydrogen peroxide in concentrations as low as 86 per cent undergoes detonation above 50°C. Solutions of 90.7 per cent peroxide have reported detonation velocities of 5500 to 6000m/sec. Mixtures of hydrogen peroxide vapour is air with as little as 35mol% H_2O_2 are reported to detonate at 1 atmosphere with a velocity of 6700m/sec. Furthermore, hydrogen peroxide, pure or in water, is readily detonable when mixed with organic materials. H_2O_2/water/ethanol has a detonation velocity of 6700m/sec. The violence of the reaction is dependent upon the amount of water present, since water acts as an energy sink for the reaction.[1]

Austria made unsuccessful attempts to use H_2O_2 as an explosive in World War I. In World War II the US Navy used it for propulsion in submarine torpedoes. Peroxide explosives have been successfully used in blasting operations. In addition to its monergolic application, hydrogen peroxide can be mixed with fuels such as methanol, ethanol, or glycerol and show detonation rates as high as 6700m/s. One of the propellant systems on the space shuttle uses the combination of hydrogen peroxide and unsymmetrical dimethylhydrazine. H_2O_2 (60 per cent) with paraformaldehyde forms a crystalline compound of high brisance and sensitive (melting point 50°C). Hydrogen peroxide (70 per cent) with diesel fuel and gelling agent also makes a good explosive. H_2O_2 (83 per cent) plus cellulose forms a gelatinous mass which is more powerful than TNT and insensitive to shock or friction. It has an ignition temperature 200°C; however, it cannot be stored over 48 hours without evolution of peroxide and loss of explosive power. Other patented peroxide explosives include H_2O_2 with water and glycerol, H_2O_2 (70 per cent with powdered boron (30 per cent), and H_2O_2 used with hexamethylenetetramine and HCl.[1]

In general, alkyl peroxides tend to be more hazardous than inorganic peroxides. Many alkyl hydroperoxides (ROOH) are reported to explode violently on jarring. Dialkyl peroxides (ROOR) are apparently more shock sensitive. Diacyl peroxides have such notations as 'explodes without apparent reason'. Dibenzoyl peroxide C_6H_5COO-$OOCC_6H_5$ is one of the few commercially available alkyl peroxides predictable enough for terrorist use.

Two peroxides can be synthesized from acetone, a dimer and a trimer. The dimer is more difficult to handle, but the trimer, triacetone triperoxide (TATP), is the suspected energetic in several terrorist incidents. The preparation of TATP described in the do-it-at-home explosive literature calls for mixing acetone and hair beach (15–25 per cent hydrogen peroxide) and adding of sulphuric acid (battery acid).[7,8] The white crystalline solid which forms after standing 24 hours explodes violently upon heating, impact, or friction. It is highly brisant, very sensitive, and detonable under water. Its reported detonation velocity is 5290m/s. It has been suggested for use in primers and detonators, but due to its volatility and sensitivity, it has not found military application.

$$CH_3CCH_3 + H_2O_2 + H_2SO_4 \rightarrow (CH_3)_2\overset{\overset{O}{|}}{C}\text{--O---O--}\overset{\overset{O}{|}}{C}(CH_3)_2$$

with $O\text{-}C(CH_3)_2\text{-}O$ bridge structure shown above

Self-igniting materials Some chemicals are so reactive to the oxygen in air or to water that they spontaneously ignite. Three parameters affect the spontaneity of ignition in air: the dryness of the air, air pressure, and temperature. Most of these chemical systems cannot be classed as explosives, but if sufficient gas pressure and heat are evolved the effect could be catastrophic. A far more important hazard, however, is the use of such devices as wireless, metal-less initiators of a more powerful explosive device.

Hydrides Phosphines, silanes, and boranes ignite on contact with air. Diphosphine (P_2H_4) a liquid at room temperature, can be made from the reaction of water with solid calcium phosphide (Ca_3P_2), which, in turn, can be formed from lime and red phosphorus. Adding water to calcium phosphide results in a mixture of phosphine and diphosphine, and a violent deflagration ensues. This reaction has been exploited in naval flares.

Only mono- and di-silanes (SiH_4 and Si_2H_6) are stable to air at room temperature. The higher silanes decompose violently. Silane gas is available in large quantities for the manufacture of microelectronic components.

Diborane (B_2H_6) is a gas available in cylinders or by the action of 85 per cent phosphoric acid on $NaBH_4$. The gas is highly toxic, and, unless it is extremely pure, it reacts with oxygen at room temperature. Borane decomposition in oxygen is extremely exothermic; therefore, boranes, such as decaborane (14) ($B_{10}H_{14}$), have been seriously considered as a component in rocket fuel.

Phosphorus White phosphorus tends to ignite with slight pressure or by contact with fuel. P_4 self-ignites in air above 34°C; as a result, it is usually stored under water. The finely divided phosphorus left on the combustible material reacts exothermically with the oxygen in air:

$P_4 + 5\ O_2 \rightarrow P_4O_{10}$

The heat of this reaction initiates the reaction between carbon disulphide and air. Drying of the phosphorus can be delayed by addition of a high-boiling hydrocarbon such as gasoline or toluene. In contrast to white phosphorus, red phosphorus is nontoxic and less sensitive. Red phosphorus bursts into flames or explodes on mild friction or impact in mixture with chlorate, permanganates, lead dioxide (PbO_2), perchlorate, and other active oxidizers ($AgNO_3$).

Miscellaneous Energetics Potassium permanganate and glycerin will ignite spontaneously after a small delay, due to the difficulty in wetting the $KMnO_4$ with viscose glycerin. Ethylene glycol, acetaldehyde, benzaldehyde, or DMSO could be used in place of glycerin. Potassium permanganate and concentrated sulphuric acid can readily inflame when in contact with fuels. $KMnO_4$ was once a common medicine for farm animals:

$$14\ KMnO_4 + 4\ C_3H_5(OH)_3 \rightarrow 7\ K_2CO_3 + 7\ Mn_2O_3 + 5\ CO_2 + 16\ H_2O$$

Conclusions

Present advances in explosive detection technology have either focused on detection of conventional military explosives or on the presence of visually recognizable components. This is an entirely reasonable approach since we have every reason to believe that terrorists bent on destruction will continue to use such dependable, high performance devices until we find a way to stop them. The task of developing effective detectors for small improvised explosive devices has been arduous, and the objective has yet to be fully accomplished. Unfortunately, once we have put such detectors in place, we should prepare to deal with a new generation of devices based on non-military explosives. The range of explosives and the packaging possibilities is staggering. To this also should be added the incendiary devices, which might trigger a more powerful material or which, with proper placement, might prove to be every bit as devastating as an explosive. A 'bomb' no longer is a recognisable sphere or pipe, nor does it necessarily need a blasting cap or squib. Every bottle, can of hair spray or shaving cream, every vacuum bottle of coffee is a possible device.

This discussion has been limited to non-military and 'exotic' explosive devices. Ignored has been the threat of traditional military explosives, weaponry, biological warfare agents, chemical warfare agents, and fire. However, it should be noted that in most of the systems discussed herein, even if the outcome were not a detonation, a vigorous fire and/or toxic fumes would result. This discussion is intended to provoke new trains of thought on possible terrorist opportunities. While some of the materials considered are thought to be too hazardous for everyday military use, terrorists may regard the level of risk as acceptable. More advanced explosive detection technology must be developed, and non-nitrogenous explosives should be targeted. Yet, now and in the foreseeable future, profiling, intelligence gathering and analysis, sound physical security practices, and common sense may remain our best security measures.

REFERENCES

1. S.M. Kaye, *Encyclopedia of Explosives and Related Items* (Dover, NJ: US Army Armament Research & Development Command; PATR-2700, 1960–78.
2. M.J. Kamlet, 'Sixth Symposium (Int'l) on Detonation', ONR ACR-211; 1976.
3. R. Meyer, *Explosives* 3rd ed. (Essen, Germany: VCH, 1987).
4. T. Urbanski, *Chemistry and Technology of Explosives* Vols. 1,2,3,4 (NY: Pergamon Press, 1964, 1965, 1967, 1984).
5. T.R. Gibbs, and A. Popolato (eds.), *LASL Explosive Property Data*, (Berkley, CA: Univ. of California Press; 1980).
6. W. Powell, *The Anarchist Cookbook* (Secaucus, NJ: Lyle Stuart Inc., 1971.
7. *Field Expedient Methods for Explosive Preparation* (Cornville, AZ: Desert Publication, 1977).
8. *Improvised Munitions Black Book* Vols.1–3 (Cornville, AZ: Desert Publications, 1981).
9. S. Lecker, *Homemade Semtex, C-4's Ugly Sister* (Boulder, CO: Paladin Press, 1991).
10. J. Galt, *The Big Bang: Improvised PETN & Mercury Fulminate* (Boulder, CO: Paladin Press, 1987).
11. Kirk-Othmer, *Encyclopedia of Chemical Technology* 3rd ed. (NY: Wiley, 1978).
12. R. Chang, and W. Tikkanen, *The Top Fifty Industrial Chemicals* (NY: Random House, 1988).
13. T.L. Davis, *The Chemistry of Powder and Explosives* (Hollywood, CA: Angriff Press, repr. of 2 vols. 1941, 1943).
14. R. Benson, *Homemade C-4: A Recipe for Survival* (Boulder, CO: Paladin Press, 1990).
15. H.D. Fair, and R.F. Walker, *Energetic Materials* Vols. I & II (NY: Plenum Press, 1977).
16. B.M. Dobratz, *LLNL Explosives Handbook, Properties of Chemical Explosives and Explosives Simultants* (Lawrence Livermore Laboratory UCRL-52997; March 1981).
17 '1990 Bomb Summary' (US Dept. of Justice, Federal Bureau of Investigation, 1990).
18. (a) K.O. Brauer, *Handbook of Pyrotechnics* (NY: Chemical Publishing Co., 1974).
    (b) H. Ellern, *Military and Civilian Pyrotechnics* (NY: Chemical Publishing Co., 1968).
    (c) J.H. McLain, *Pyrotechnics* (The Franklin Inst., 1980).
19. R.B. Hopler, Hercules Powder Co. Kenvil, NJ, internal report, July 1964.
20. (a) F.T. Maggs, and D. Sutton, *Trans. Faraday Soc.* 54 (1958), p.1861.
    (b) D.B. Broughton; R.L. Wentworth, *J.Am.Chem.Soc.* 69 (1947), p.741.
21. W. Bannister, presentation at National Energetic Materials Workshop, 14–17 April 1992.
22. D.S. Burgess, J.N. Murphy, N.E. Hanna and R.W. Van Dolah, 'Large-Scale Studies of Gas Detonations', US Bureau of Mines, Report No.7196, 1968.

The Nuclear Dimension

ANDREW LOEHMER

In the light of continued nuclear proliferation and terrorist threats, the feasibility of terrorist organizations gaining access to weapons of mass destruction has to be analyzed anew and in depth. Although guerrillas and terrorist have more or less refrained from nuclear weaponry, export controls on nuclear technology (not only on behalf of the dissolution of the former Soviet Union) need to be enforced on a larger scale, and nuclear reactor safety has to be guaranteed.

The objective of this paper is to outline the feasibility and probability of terrorists gaining access to and using nuclear weapons (biological or chemical weapons shall merely be touched on) in favour of achieving their political or other aims. Since this topic is a very specific one, literature is rather limited in comparison to other themes related to terrorism. This is to say that the paper is mainly based on books, essays and articles published in the late 1970s and early 1980s when nuclear terrorism was broadly discussed. The author, however, has tried to analyse and circumscribe more recent developments as well even though material was difficult to find.

The paper does not claim to have highlighted every single point of interest, rather it wants to give the reader a brief overview on the range and consequences of nuclear terrorism in particular and its implications on the success of terrorist organisations within the international system in general. Furthermore it serves as a statement that nuclear safety in terms of preventing nuclear attacks and nuclear theft on the one hand, and the containment of nuclear proliferation as a means of minimizing the possibility for terrorist organisations and state-regimes gaining technological material on the other hand, deserve the utmost attention and serious countermeasures.

1. What about Nuclear Terrorism?

This paper does not deal with nuclear terrorism as Thomas Schelling once defined it – namely being the 'balance of nuclear terror' between the major nuclear weapon states[1] – but rather refers to terrorist groups going nuclear. One might have the following situation in mind: a terrorist organisation has been successful in hijacking two tactical nuclear weapons from a NATO aircraft and blackmails the British and US governments to pay $500,000 within seven days or – if not – either a city in the United Kingdom or in the United States will be bombed. This scenario is drawn from the James Bond movie *Thunderball* released in 1964 and to that time and even now seems far-fetched (although in 1992 the movie *Under Siege* touched on the same possible threat). Yet an operation like that can never be excluded, although the possibility of successful results is not very likely. However, nuclear blackmail can manifest itself in other forms, for example in the way that terrorists achieve nuclear weapon technology from nuclear weapon states or by theft and in consequence put pressure on specific target groups or states. Slightly different, but similar in concept, is the threat posed by terrorists with biological and chemical warfare capability. As they stand they are – with similar devastating consequences – the 'nuclear weapons of the poor'. As the paper in the first place discusses the nuclear aspect of terrorism, biological and chemical weapons will be observed briefly in a later section.

In his book *The Absolute Weapon*, written in 1946, Bernard Brodie pointed out 'the new potentialities which the atomic bomb gives to sabotage'.[2] Thus, already over 45 years ago a threat of 'nuclear' terrorism has been recognised. However, not before the mid-1970s have politicians and academics shown genuine concern about substate actors' and terrorist organizations' use of nuclear material (esp. weaponry).

Why, then, has nuclear terrorism captured so much attention from 1974 on[3] up till now? The answer covers a broad range of possibilities of which the most important seem to be as follows:[4] First, the socialization of terrorists has included an exposure to military strategies that unscrupulously weigh the mass destruction of civilians. Second, the spread of nuclear technology has made the needed material (for the construction of devices) more accessible. Third, the numerous personnel employed in the 'nuclear sector' might lead to either an attempt to construct a bomb or the selling of know-how to other regimes or organizations for financial advantage. Finally, the Atoms for Peace programme which led to a declassification of a vast amount of material from the US Atomic Energy Commission on the one hand, and the proliferation of literature – such as books, articles, essays and speeches – intended to warn the world of the growing problem on the other hand challenged terrorists with the possibility of going nuclear. Thus, Albert Wohlstetter concludes: 'It is even barely possible – as those who have recently warned us to recognize – that advertising the technical feasibility will raise the probability'.[5] Analysing the amount of literature written on the topic of nuclear terrorism, one can differentiate between two schools of thought – the 'realistic school' and the 'faith bloc'. While the former examines motives, technical feasibility and historical evidence, the latter seems to accept the likelihood of nuclear terrorism as a matter of fatalism faith (in the nuclear capability).[6] This distinction will not be emphasized throughout the paper but gives an idea of the existence of different academic or other approaches to the threat.

However, all the authors surveyed believe that the threat of nuclear terrorism is a product of two current developments in world politics; the proliferation of civilian and military nuclear technology and the burgeoning of terrorism, both of which have reached unprecedented levels.[7] Brian Jenkins rightly points out that nuclear terrorism combines 'the two darkest fears of our era: the fear of nuclear destruction and the fear of rising terrorism'.[8] Even so, nuclear terrorism leaves a somewhat paradoxical impression for terrorism is usually considered to be the 'weapon of the weak' and nuclear power, on the other hand, is regarded as the hallmark and symbol of might and 'super power' in international relations.[9] It does not follow, however, that the threat posed by nuclear terrorism should be underestimated, but rather that it should be given serious treatment in theory and in practice.

In dealing with nuclear terrorism, especially when projecting it to terrorist organisations rather than to states (although states can be terrorist as well), it is useful to recall Paul Wilkinson's typology of international terror perpetrators: he distinguishes between the nationalist terrorists, the ideological terrorists, the religious fanatics, the single issue fanatics, and the state – sponsored international terrorist.[10] Moreover it should be kept in mind – while researching the topic of nuclear terrorism – what the term 'terrorism' basically encompasses. As Wilkinson puts it 'one major complexity [in the analysis of terrorism] has been the problem of definition.[11] He goes on by stating that now 'there is general recognition that terrorism is a specific method of struggle rather than a synonym for political violence or insurgency' and that it is generally accepted 'that what distinguishes terrorism from other forms of violence is the deliberate and systematic use of coercive intimidation'.[12] Applied to nuclear terrorism it means that terrorists might test fissionable material, attack nuclear facilities, use radioactive material to contaminate or create alarming nuclear hoaxes.

The rapid growth of the civilian nuclear industry, increasing traffic in plutonium-enriched uranium and radioactive waste material, the spread of nuclear technology not only in the Western world, have all increased the opportunities for terrorists to engage in some type of nuclear action. The perpetrators – ranging from common criminals, disgruntled guerrillas, employees, political (anti-nuclear) extremists, or simply authentic lunatics – may 'try to take advantage of the fear that the word "nuclear" generates without taking risks or making the investment necessary to steal plutonium and build a working atom bomb'.[13] A well publicized hoax could be even more threatening as the actual possession of a nuclear weapon, as could be a terrorist attack on a nuclear facility, even if the individual or group did not achieve the intended objective. Any incidents involving nuclear material or facilities are certain to receive extensive media coverage. It therefore follows as a logical conclusion that the International Task Force on Prevention of Nuclear Terrorism at its conference in late 1985 added the prevention of nuclear terrorism as the fourth overriding imperative dominating mankind's efforts to exploit and control the energy of the atom.[14] The threat exists due to the growth of the nuclear power industry, its vulnerabilities to theft or attack by terrorist organizations and because of the increasing flow of 'high technology' information. To what extent this existing threat is credible is mainly connected to the question about the terrorists' *feasibility* and *probability* on going nuclear.

2. Feasibility of Terrorists Going Nuclear

When Guy Fawkes attempted to blow up the English Parliament in 1605 with 36 barrels of gunpowder it illustrated well the employment of state-of-the-art technology for terrorist motives. Since the early twentieth century, technological advancement primarily in the industrialized nations has occurred and a greater pace than at any time before. Technologies with mass destruction and mass casualty potential have been widely developed and deployed by the military around the world. One result of this proliferation of technology is that for the first time in history terrorists now have obtainable a broad spectrum of means that carry catastrophic consequences – not only in terms of biological and chemical weapons but foremost in the nuclear field.[15] The spectrum of mischievous actions by terrorists who are on their way to pursue a potential nuclear threat includes

> the creation of potentially alarming hoaxes, acts of low-level symbolic sabotage, the occupation or seizure of nuclear facilities, acts of serious sabotage aimed at causing widespread casualties and damage, thefts of nuclear material, armed attacks on nuclear weapons storage sites, thefts of nuclear weapons, the dispersal of radio active contaminants, the manufacture of homemade nuclear weapons, and the detonation of such devices.[16]

2.1 Ways of Obtaining Fissile Material (SNM)

There exist at least five ways for terrorists obtaining the fissile material for building a nuclear device: separation of plutonium from irradiated light or heavy water reactor fuel in own facilities; theft of fissile material during transport; obtaining the needed material from a black market; material through state-sponsoring; or theft of an intact nuclear weapon. Since the latter three ways will be described in subsequent sections, I shall only concentrate on the former two.

Intense concern has grown in recent years over the increasing amount of plutonium and high-enriched uranium which is being produced and stockpiled. It is generally acknowledged that as larger amounts of fissile material are used in civilian nuclear activity the probability of terrorist thefts increases. It is also widely recognized that both plutonium 238 and 239 as well as highly enriched uranium 235 could easily be used in a crude nuclear device. However, to separate the plutonium, terrorists need a processing facility and to build that facility they need a site and the planning and design of the facility by architects, engineers and chemists. Moreover, the need for all the other materials for the construction of such a site would require considerable money and technical capability resources. Separating plutonium, therefore, does not appear to be a credible route to a terrorist nuclear weapon capability.[17]

Although power reactors, other nuclear fuel cycle facilities and transport of spent nuclear fuel are mainly seen as the targets for terrorist attacks and sabotage, they also provide the source for 'nuclear theft'.[18] Whereas an attack on power reactors and nuclear fuel sites is possible but highly difficult, stealing fissile material – while it is being transported – seems more likely. According to Brian Jenkins '[t]he lack of a nuclear black market and the unlikelihood that governments will provide terrorists with nuclear material leave thefts as the most likely means by which terrorists will achieve nuclear material'.[19] Terrorist organisations themselves might try to steal the material overtly but nowadays the security environment would bring terrorists up against a higher level of safeguard in their attempt to achieve weapons-grade nuclear fuel. As a consequence terrorists could commission others to carry out the theft on their behalf; a terrorist group in one specific country might want nuclear material but simply lacks the means or connections to carry out an operation.[20] The disadvantages, however, of a commissioned theft include uncertainty about the reliability of its agents and could involve a problem of provoking an enormous recovery effort.

To avoid the latter inconvenience terrorists could try to acquire the needed material covertly with the assistance of inside confederate.[21] Since it is doubtful, as stated above, that terrorists will possess a capability for enriching uranium or extracting plutonium from irradiated fuel, they will have to seek it in a readily utilisable form. Enrichment facilities, fuel fabrication, fuel reprocessing, weapons-fabrication facilities and research facilities possess highly enriched material. The theft, however, would nevertheless only be carried out by those individuals or groups that did know how to use the 'stuff'.[22] They might be able to launch a commando-like operation or to offer a large amount of money for high-grade nuclear explosive material. In the light of this threat and the assumption that in the year 2000 there will exist twice as much civilian plutonium as the amount presently deployed in nuclear weapon programmes and stockpiles,[23] the safeguard system has to be enforced and improved and the physical protection of nuclear material – as laid down in the UN Convention on the Physical Protection of Nuclear Material[24] – has to be underlined. If not, the probability of terrorists obtaining weapon-grade material will definitely increase.

2.2 Construction of the Lethal Weapon

> The most probable application of nuclear terrorism is the occupation of a nuclear facility, establishing a hostage situation. Theft of a weapon or weapons-grade material is the next most probably occurrence, while dispersal and, finally, *fabrication of a bomb are the least*.[25]

Even if Walter Laqueur points out in his conclusion that the 'popular idea of a nuclear device produced in a garage and transported on a tricycle seems to belong for the time being to the realms of fantasy',[26] and Brian Jenkins only sees 'few terrorists [. . .] possess the requisite technical skills identified by experts', since most terrorists derive from the departments of social sciences and humanities rather than from the engineering or physics side,[27] it has been estimated – depending on the nature of the basic nuclear material at hand – that to some extent, a clandestine nuclear device could be constructed by a single individual, an even more credible bomb by only three or four.[28] However, the development and subsequent refinement of nuclear, chemical and biological weapons has resulted in the credible possibility that a single individual could develop a capacity of causing mass destruction.[29] At a conference in June 1985 experts ruled out the fact that nuclear, biological, or chemical incidents were impossible,[30] and agreed that increased state-sponsorship put at the terrorists' disposal more resources – such as intelligence, money, and technical expertise.[31]

Now that we know that terrorists are capable of constructing a nuclear device how do they do it and what do they need to do it? To fabricate nuclear weapons there are two crucial ingredients: one is the fissile material, uranium or plutonium of sufficient enrichment purity,[32] the other is the personnel with the engineering knowledge and skill. Since nuclear power electricity is likely to grow within the next years, most nations will eventually have within their national borders reactors that produce plutonium as an intended or an unintended by-product. The chemical separation of the weapon-grade plutonium from the spent reactor fuel is a process that will go hand in hand with the industrial capability of most industrialized, and even underdeveloped states (especially if foreign companies are available to do it on contract).[33] The design and fabrication of a bomb is then assumed to be a task that any of these nations can do without outside help. It follows that terrorists in this development face two opportunities: on the one hand they have more fissile material around the world available to them for theft and, on the other hand increased state-sponsorship may provide individuals or groups with the material. Moreover Schelling concludes that 'because not every step in this "nuclear fuel cycle" will be done at central locations under continuous heavy armed guard, there is a possibility of theft or hijacking of the kind of material of which nuclear bombs can be made.'[34]

> Whatever opinions anyone may have about the likelihood that an individual or very small group of people would actually steal nuclear materials and use them to make fission bombs, those opinions should not be based on a presumption that all types of fission bombs are very difficult to make.[35]

The fact is that not even high-technology nuclear devices have to be built to render devastating consequences. They are easier and quicker to construct and pose significant destructive effects. A nuclear explosive in a 'limited range' of 1000 tons could annihilate the Capitol or blow up the World Trade Center towers.[36] We must remember that nuclear explosives are more damaging than any other comparable weapon, for they produce energy in form of blast, heat and radiation.[37]

However, it is unlikely that terrorist organizations would build their own bomb. Given their often strict revolutionary agenda, their lack of cohesiveness over a long construction period and their very limited – if any – possibility of producing the material on their own, other ways of threatening the target groups or states are available (sometimes easier) and seem more convincing. They shall be dealt with below.

2.3. Theft of an Intact Nuclear Weapon

At first glance, the most direct means of acquiring a private nuclear capability would seem to be to steal an intact nuclear weapon. Although security levels at nuclear weapon sites and depots are high, it would be foolish to discount the possibility of a terrorist attack against nuclear weapons, for example, in Europe. Such an attack, according to a panel of experts, would have a very high public and political impact.[38] An attack on storage sites or deployed forces could raise to a politically unacceptable level of the public's anxiety where nuclear weapons are concerned.[39] A detonation of a stolen nuclear weapon, however, would not be needed by a terrorists in achieving public panic (there are other means of doing so which will be discussed later on).

US nuclear weapons in Europe, especially tactical nuclear weapons, have been regarded as being the most likely target for a terrorist theft. First, these weapons constitute a set of potential targets in areas where terrorists, usually with a strident anti-Americanism as an element of their perspective, have operated and are operating[40] and, second, not all of the tactical nuclear weapons are provided with the so-called permissive action link (PAL), a locking system to prevent terrorists detonating a stolen weapon or dismantling it to obtain nuclear material.[41] A panel of experts, therefore, in 1985 suggested an extension of PALs to all nuclear devices in order to prevent terrorist organizations of using the stolen material.[42] Yet even today nuclear weapons are reported to have been exported from the former Soviet Union that lack the important PAL.[43] Even in the light of disarmament between the US and Russia, decisive numbers of nuclear devices (including strategic nuclear weapons since they are all provided with PALs) remain that still give terrorists the opportunity for a potential theft.[44]

The mitigating conditions, however, which even in the event of the successful acquisition of a nuclear weapon could hinder the direct use of firing of it – such as the PALs, the involvement of a complex series of steps in the arming procedure, and so forth – combined with the fact that 'only a few nuclear weapons are truly manportable' and the infrastructure of the terrorist organizations for storing or even launching the device is weak,[45] do not seem to underline the fear of a nuclear weapon attack by terrorists. But, as Mullen puts it '[u]nauthorized possession of a military nuclear device would be a matter of grave concern. No matter that the group possessing the device may not be able to make it function.[46]

2.4 Sabotage of Nuclear Fuel Sites

In the last twenty years increases in both the total volume of terrorist incidents worldwide and the casualties resulting from such incidents have prompted renewed concern that terrorists might attack a nuclear facility. Apart from other reasons that have already been named above one of the objectives of the terrorists on the nuclear field is merely the sabotage or destruction of the facility itself.[47] According to observers, the initiative to sabotage a nuclear reactor has already been taken.[48] To date, there have occurred perhaps six attacks on nuclear powerplants in France, South Africa, Argentina, the Philippines, and Spain.[49] Fortunately, all of the reactors were in the early stages of construction and not operational.[40] According to three experts (Albright, Hirsch, Hoffman), the security of nuclear reactors against terrorist attacks has been seriously compromised. As Hirsch observes, there is a distinct tendency in the field of nuclear safeguards and security to protect against threats that are relatively easy to protect against and to ignore those that are more difficult.[51] For instance, both Hirsch and Hoffman point out that the Nuclear Research Council's 'design basis threat' assumes that adversaries would carry out an assault on foot, with only as much explosives as they could carry and with the assistance of only one insider.[52] It does not recognise the possibility of the use of vehicles in the form of a truck bomb. This is despite the 1984 Sandia National Laboratories study, which was conducted in response to the rash of vehicular bombing, in particular the 1983 truck bombing of the US Marine camp at Beirut airport. It concluded that 'the use of conventional explosives against nuclear facilities would result in unacceptable damage to vital reactor systems'.[53] Specific reference was given to truck bombing, when the reports acknowledged that a small explosive device at a close distance or a larger device further away could easily cause such severe damage.[54] Despite security efforts being made, reactors will remain vulnerable to this potentially devastating type of attack.

The same intransigence has occurred over the greatest threat to nuclear facilities: the 'insider' threat.[55] Hirsch regards this as a 'dual' threat, fearing both theft and sabotage. Of particular concern in this respect is the practice of publishing Probability Risk Assessments (PRAs) which are seen to be 'virtual road maps for saboteurs'.[56]

However, since the Chernobyl catastrophe in 1986, the severity of a reactor meltdown (in case of a terrorist act) cannot be underestimated and has at the same time shown that terrorist sabotage on nuclear facilities can be viewed as one of the most dangerous and more likely forms of 'high-level' nuclear terrorism.[57]

2.5. Radiological Dispersal

Radiological terrorism may be defined as the malevolent dispersal of radiological material. These substances can be found in gases, liquids or in solid form and are used for medical, industrial and research purposes. They may also be found as reactor waste or fission products. Although the opportunities for this form of nuclear terrorism are perhaps more numerous than any other form of nuclear material terrorist threat, there have been surprisingly few incidents to date.[58] Though the details are sketchy, the most celebrated incident occurred in Austria, when in 1974 a railroad car was contaminated with what was believed to be either indium 113m or iodine 131.[59] Similar accidents have taken place in France and twice in Austin (Texas).[60] Fortunately, the substances involved in the described occurrences were not highly radioactive. However, if plutonium 238 or 239 were to be used, the results would certainly be fatal.[61]

What sets radiological terrorism apart from many other forms of conventional and nuclear terrorism is its effect. Unlike the explosion of a nuclear device, a radiological dispersal act does not have an instantaneous and obviously destructive effect. Unless the dosage is massive, the victims may not even know that they have been exposed to such toxic substances and may not feel the effects until weeks, perhaps even years or decades later.

> The plutonium dispersal weapon is, simple, not a weapon of mass destruction. This is not to minimize the other characteristics of such a weapon which include radiological contamination and the potential for causing life-shortening through induction of cancers in individuals 15 to 30 years following exposure.[62]

The success of this type of terrorism, however, depends on the terrorists' objectives, the effectiveness of the 'attack' and the public's reaction.[63] Nevertheless, experts have pointed out that the threat of radiological contamination may attract terrorists since it demands the least requirements compared to other forms of nuclear terrorism.[64]

3. Probability of Terrorists Going Nuclear

As the above stated has shown terrorists do have the technical and intellectual know-how, in short meet the conditions of feasibility, to go nuclear. The question that has to be addressed now is if it is probable that terrorists, once they have gained the capability of using nuclear weapons or material, would actually make use of it in the pursuit of achieving their objectives.

3.1. Intent and Psychological Motivations

> It would be a great mistake to assume that political terrorists will conform to some minimum standard of rationality and humanity.[65]

Fortunately, nuclear terrorism has up till now not become a *direct* threat or danger. With the exception of minor incidents, in which terrorists temporarily occupied nonoperational nuclear plants in Spain and Argentina, and a truck-driver with his station-wagon crashed into the territory of the Three Mile Island plant in Pennsylvania, terrorists have not attacked nuclear facilities, stolen nuclear weapons or fissile material, nor even committed credible nuclear hoaxes. Yet, observers have pointed out that there have been important changes in international terrorist activity, in nuclear weapons technology, and in the availability of nuclear material that might lessen the constraints that have thus far kept terrorist organizations from entering the nuclear realm.

Many experts share the opinion that the primary attraction to terrorists in going nuclear is not necessarily the fact that nuclear weapons enable them to cause mass casualties, but rather than the words 'atomic' and 'nuclear' automatically generate fear and perhaps even panic in the public.[66] Terrorism does not necessarily have to be linked to mindless violence. It can be described as a campaign of violence designed to inspire fear, to create an atmosphere of alarm which causes the population to exaggerate the strength and importance of the terrorist movement.

> Terrorism is violence for effect. Terrorists choreograph violence to achieve maximum publicity. Terrorism is theater.[67]

As mass casualties simply may not serve the terrorists' goals and could alienate the population ('Terrorists want a lot of people *watching*, not a lot of people *dead*'), terrorists operate on the principle of the minimum force necessary.[68] Moreover, according to Hoffman, the vast majority of the terrorists are 'not particularly innovative'.[69] Although radical in their politics, their operations seem to be more conservative, in short, they are likely to stick to the rules they know and have been working to.[70] It follows, that if terrorists had a nuclear capability, they would be more likely to gesture it as a threat than detonate it. The principal object is obtaining a nuclear weapon would, therefore, be to blackmail the leaders of a society into meeting demands and to threaten the lives and effectiveness of the principal authorities concerned in dealing with terrorist activity (i.e., government and police). Yet the translation of the enormous coercive power that a nuclear device would give a terrorist group into concrete political gains poses difficulties. First, the terrorists would have to establish the credibility of the threat. As a matter of fact, these blackmailers are reluctant to mount threats that they are not prepared to execute if their demands are not being met.[71] Secondly, the terrorists would have to persuade the targeted government that it has an incentive to negotiate.[72] In short, 'going nuclear' presents even sophisticated terrorists with serious operational and political problems.

Although in the recent past nuclear terror seemed more attractive as a threat than as an action, the probability of a terrorist organisation using the lethal weapon cannot be ruled out entirely. Why? The character of terrorism itself can change. This is to say that first, ethnic and religious fanaticism, for example, can easily allow terrorists to overcome the psychological barriers to mass murder.[73] Second, transnational terro-rism has increased its lethality:[74] after hostage taking and killing in the 1970s, terrorists did not hesitate to assassinate 241 US Marines in 1983 with a truck-bomb in Beirut or bomb an Air India Boeing 747 killing 329 persons or blasting the Pan Am Boeing 747 over Lockerbie (270 deaths) in 1988. The latest bombings of the Israeli embassy in Buenos Aires in March 1992, of the World Trade Center in New York in February 1993 and of several locations in Bombay (leaving over 300 dead and over 1000 injured) show that the moral threshold diminishes permanently. And finally, a greater terrorist activity under state-sponsorship.[75] In other words, nuclear terrorists can act undercover while depriving the threat of retaliation, in case of having exploded a nuclear device, to a level of a certain security dilemma for the responding party.

3.2. Terrorist Nuclear Attack: A Scenario

When the twin towers of the World Trade Center were hit by a con-ventional explosive device in early March 1992,[76] not only the citizens of New York but the rest of the world held their breath. Despite the fact that casualties had resulted from this unscupulous terrorist attack, pre-sumptions might have come forward of what could have happened if a crude nuclear bomb would have been planted in the building. The re-cent and relevant developments in the fields of not only weapon technology, but of transport and communications, and the emergence of transnational terrorism – involving terrorists of different nationalities planning, training for, and executing acts of political terrorism – have enhanced the danger of nuclear terrorism to a significant extent.[77] Just imagine the following situation: a terrorist organization – in our case the Hizbollah – has somehow planted a nuclear device of considerable yield in the World Trade Center (at the very location of the detonated con-ventional explosive) and is blackmailing the US government to release a certain number of its follow terrorists and to coerce Israel to pull out of its occupied territories within one month. In case of not fulfilling the demands the nuclear weapon would be detonated. The Armageddon takes place,[78] for the Hizbollah is – as I presupposed in my scenario – so fanatic that it takes into account its longterm destruction and the end of their pursuit for political objectives.

How to respond? Undoubtedly the United States would succeed in destroying the terrorist movement, once it found out who was re-sponsible for the lethal act. But the usual and trained response for a nuclear attack – namely 'massive retaliation' as part of their nuclear deterrence strategy – would fail.[79] On the one hand, the US could not precisely launch a nuclear retaliation act against a Hizbollah camp, since they are in different states and perhaps even in their own.[80] On the other hand, if the US did get to know that the nuclear strike was sponsored by Iran, a nuclear attack on their homeland could not entirely be justified (for it was not the perpetrator). In both cases the victim-state would have to face the dilemma of perhaps initiating/provoking a nuclear world war.

This scenario shows – even of low probability – the threats, dangers, helplessness, devastation and disorder that would be brought about in case of active nuclear terrorism.

4. Influencing Factors on Nuclear Terrorism

4.1. Proliferation of Nuclear Hard and Software

In a world where still about 40,000 nuclear warheads with a total destructive power more than a million times that of Hiroshima are deployed,[81] where the dissolution of the Soviet Union threw open the question of who is in control of what and what happens to the amount of nuclear weapons in the three other former Soviet republics,[82] where at least 20 states possess or can produce at least two types of weapons – whether nuclear, biological or chemical – and their delivery systems,[83] and where the 'nuclear club' is about to grow every year,[84] the enforcement of the non-proliferation regime – namely the Treaty on the Nonproliferation of Nuclear Weapons (148 members as of mid-1992) – or better its extension beyond 1995 seems to be an urgent need.[85]

The growing diffusion of knowledge about nuclear technology, possibilities for illegal transfer of nuclear material,[86] lax security procedures, and – as already stated above – the increasing sophistication of terrorist methods cannot rule out the possibility of nuclear terrorism in our lifetime. The greatest challenge, however, for the non-proliferation regime lies in the risk posed by the new nuclear weapon states, especially Belorussia, Kazakhstan, and Ukraine. Not only could they – against their agreements – in a crisis-situation (i.e., with Russia) remain nuclear, moreover they could – because of a desperate need for cash – sell their tactical nuclear weapons or other fissile material (after the dismantling of other nuclear weapons) to third-state parties who might as well sponsor terrorists.[87] Or their nuclear experts might 'sell themselves' to other states to earn more money.[88] Whatever might happen, these risks of nuclear proliferation will continue to keep the international community on tenterhooks for a long time to come.

4.2. The Black Market

One possibility for states or terrorist groups to obtain nuclear material, technological know-how or tools which enable them to build a nuclear bomb lies in illegal transactions. In the past these transactions remained of minor influence and have not yet produced a black market. However, all the elements needed for a well-functioning market are available. The continued and enlarged proliferation and use of civilian nuclear energy[89] might therefore enhance the danger of a rising black market, as long as the trade with fissile or weapons-grade material is not being surrendered worldwide. In the light of the new nuclear republics of the former Soviet Union (see earlier end notes 81–88), the reckless 'greed-behaviour' of weapon-trusts or other companies[90] in the private sector and a level of corruption in certain nation-states,[91] the avoidance of a nuclear black market and illegal transaction seems highly unlikely.

4.3. Physical Protection and Safeguards

With respect to the assaults put forward on nuclear fuel sites and transports one must conclude that they are insufficiently secured against attacks and that the fissile material is still too vulnerable to theft. The planned security and safety measures do not meet the required needs, but rather reflect the financial and organizational capabilities of the owner.[92] Improvements are feasible only at the cost of the citizen's freedom.[93] Rossnagel, therefore, concludes that a worldwide ban on the use of weapon-grade nuclear material should be agreed upon.[94] According to an article in the *International Herald Tribune*,[95] however, the Nuclear Regulatory Commission (NRC) wants to re-evaluate the threat truck-bombs pose to nuclear reactors in the light of the World Trade Center event and an incident earlier in 1993 in which a person crashed his station wagon through the fence of the Three Mile Island plant in Pennsylvania.

Since this paper does not deal with the problems of preventing nuclear terrorism, the status of safeguards will be discussed merely in a few words.

At present, multilateral safeguards are concerned with deterring the proliferation of nuclear weapons among nations. The cornerstone of this regime is the Non-Proliferation Treaty. Within the treaty, non-nuclear weapon states agree to open their nuclear facilities for International Atomic Energy Agency (IAEA) inspection and in exchange receive civilian nuclear technology from nuclear states. The IAEA's task is to deter national diversions of nuclear materials from civilian uses to military programmes via threat of 'timely' detection. Unfortunately, not every signatory to the NPT has agreed on the IAEA safeguard system. Without this control-mechanism the strength of the non-proliferation regime might well be doubted. However, Moglewer observes that the actual effectiveness of the IAEA in terms of overall safeguards sense is questionable, especially with respect to the threat of nuclear terrorism.[96] The IAEA safeguards rest on the assumption that states and terrorists are in continual conflict with each other. Consequently, the possibility of co-operation between states and terrorist organizations is not addressed. Furthermore, the IAEA's statistical methods of measuring national diversions are inaccurate at best. The agency could not even detect a diversion of SNM from a medium to a large size nuclear facility.[97] The IAEA has very limited authority to verify the accuracy of national material accounting methods and controls and virtually no influence over the safeguards concerning physical safety of SNM at nuclear powerplants or other facilities. In sum, the IAEA's primary concern is not one of regulation but of monitoring and auditing.[98]

5. The Impact of Chemical and Biological Weapons

In the press the dispersal of deadly chemical or biological agents is frequently treated as no more difficult than dumping the material in a community water supply. So done, mass casualties are automatically expected to be the result. Rarely, however, would this be the case. The efficient dispersal of a potential agent of mass destruction could be a problem not to be underestimated for anyone contemplating such an act.

Chemical Agents

When a terrorist group decides to make use of chemical agents,[99] no matter what method of dissemination is chosen, losses during this process will occur which are usually quite large: at least, it may be assumed that 90 per cent of the dispersed agent will not reach the intended target in doses sufficient enough to cause casualties.[100] According to Mullen, several methods of dispersing chemical agents can be discussed: contamination of bulk food supplies; generation of gases in enclosed spaces with volatile agents; generation of aerosols in enclosed spaces with nonvolatile agents; and dispersal with explosives.[101] While the first three of these mechanisms would probably occur under covert conditions, the last would have to be pursued overtly. It follows that if a terrorist organization were to attempt an attack on a larger scale, such an attempt would need to be based on the logistical and material resources required to launch this kind of attack effectively (i.e., artillery shells or short range missiles). A chemical agent attack on a select population of individuals, on the other hand, is manageable by a single terrorist. Summing up, the clandestine chemical attack does not appear a viable method of producing a very high casualty rate, although an event which resulted in a few hundred fatalities could certainly be characterised as mass destruction.

In the light of the January 1993 signature of the Chemical Weapons Convention in Paris – regarded as the most ambitious multilateral arms control agreement ever, which prohibits the development, production, acquisition, transfer, and stockpiling of chemical weapons, also prohibits the encouragement of other nations to conduct any of these activities, and requires all parties to declare and destroy all their chemical weapon stockpiles and production facilities[102] – there is hope that at least terrorists will no longer be able to obtain chemical agents that pose a potential threat against populations.

Biological Agents

Compared to the chemical ones these agents are more lethal. An effective dispersal is for the most part limited to aerosolization. At the same time the aerosol dissemination of almost any biological agent poses the most significant problem since it is not certain that the agent will survive long enough to infect the intended target.[103] It might happen that the mechanical process of the aerosolisation kills a significant proportion of the pathogenic agent. Instead:

> But if an adversary possessed some basic understanding of meteorology, the biological characteristics of the agent he chose to employ, the requirements for and affects to aerosolization, was careful in the selection of the target population, and was aware of the various temporal and spatial conditions which would affect the aerosol dispersal of a particular organism, a *significant threat* could arise.[104]

However, bacteria can also be dispersed by means of explosions or can be fed into a building's air conditioning or ventilation system (imagine the World Trade Center incident with biological agents!). This kind of warfare is extremely attractive to terrorists for it is relatively easy and cheap to manufacture these deadly viruses and microorganisms and they are highly suitable for covert dispersal.[105] And Mullen even assures us that 'the resources required to mount a credible mass destruction threat with a biological weapon are trivial compared to those required for a credible explosive nuclear threat'.[106]

6. Conclusion: The Unpredictable Terrorist Nuclear Threat

Undoubtedly nuclear terrorism is a very specific pattern of terrorism which does not seem to fit into the common scheme of terrorist activity.

While the terrorist's threat is normally based on some kind of guerrilla ideology, terrorism is often considered to be 'the weapon of the weak and few'. However, with the technological, economic, political and ideological changes in the world, the terrorist's attitude towards his/her objectives and the means needed to achieve them have altered as well. Unfortunately, as has been pointed out in the paper, the world had to watch a 'dual development' in the international arena: on the one hand, nuclear proliferation and the greed of many states to gain access to the 'power weapon' made the availability of nuclear material not only easier but even more interesting.[107] And, on the other hand, terrorism itself, despite the fact that it got more involved on the transnational level, became increasingly lethal. There still exist enough terrorist movements, however, that have not yet turned away from their basic thoughts on how to achieve political objectives. In that respect the use of a nuclear weapon would in no way fit into their concept. As Jenkins has put it, not the death of the population, but rather their attention should be the strategy's outcome. Terrorists fear alienating their perceived constituents. Moreover, there may be self-imposed constraints that derive from moral considerations or political calculations, in the sense that some terrorists might regard indiscriminate violence as immoral. Even so, possessing a weapon of mass destruction would definitely go hand in hand with a blackmailing position.

For the near-term future we are perhaps more likely to deal with terrorist threats of chemical of biological contamination. Over the long-term we might witness an increased use of chemical warfare and later even nuclear weapons.[108] Yet, it is not so much the credibility of a nuclear threat posed by the terrorists that causes deep worries. It is rather the unawareness of target states or groups about the implications of a terrorist group possessing a usable nuclear device[109] and the additional fear of their unpredictability of using it.

As shown throughout the paper terrorists are definitely capable of going nuclear. And although not very likely the probability of doing so cannot be completely ruled out. In the light of rising ethnic tensions, nationalist ideology and religious fundamentalism – all of which can be state-sponsored – terrorism can lose its former pretentions and very quickly – on the basis of incompatible value systems – turn into what nobody ever wants to think about: the Nuclear Armageddon.

NOTES

1. The mere existence of nuclear capabilities and facilities poses the threat of terror.

See e.g., one of the numerous publications of Schelling referring to this topic; Thomas C. Schelling, 'Who Will Have the bomb?' *International Security* 1/1 (Summer 1976), pp.87–8.

2. So cited in Augustus R. Norton, 'Introduction' in Norton and Martin H. Greenberg, (eds.): *Studies in Nuclear Terrorism* (Boston: G.K. Hall & Co., 1979) p.3.
3. In 1974 Theodore Taylor, a distinguished nuclear weapons engineer, and Mason Willrich with their book *Nuclear Theft: Risks and Safeguards* first opened the eyes of policymakers and informed citizens of the dangers and challenges of nuclear terrorism.
4. Compare ibid., pp.3–4.
5. So cited in Norton (note 2), p.4.
6. See ibid.; pp.5–8.
7. See Brian Michael Jenkins , *The Likelihood of Nuclear Terrorism* (Santa Monica, CA: RAND Corp. Paper, No.P.-7119: July 1985), p.3. For a good and concise analysis on nuclear terrorism, see Harald Müller, 'Nuklearterrorismus invermeidlicher begleiter der Lichespaltung?' in Wolfgang Gessenharter and Helmut Fröchling (ed.), *Atomwirtschaft und innere Sicherheit* (Baden-Baden: Nomos Verlag, 1989), pp.141–70.
8. Ibid.,p.1.
9. See March C. Hutchinson, 'Defining Future Threats: Terrorists and Nuclear Proliferation' in: Norton and Greenberg (note 2), p. 147.
10. See Paul Wilkinson, 'Terrorism: An International Research Agenda?'; in Wilkinson and Alasdair Stewart, *Contemporary Research on Terrorism* (Aberdeen UP, 1989), p.xiii.
11. Ibid.; p.xi.
12. Ibid.; for another appropriate definition of the term terrorism see Edward Mickolus: 'Trends in Transnational Terrorism' in Marius H. Livingstone, *International Terrorism in the Contemporary World* (Westport, CT and London, UK: Greenwood Press, 1978), p.44. He defines it as '[t]he use, or threat of use, of anxiety-inducing extranormal violence for political purposes by an individual or group, whether acting for or in opposition to established governmental authority, when such action is intended to influence the attitudes and behaviour of a target group wider than the immediate victims and when, through the nationality or foreign ties of its perpetrators, its location, the nature of its institutional or human victims, or the mechanics of its resolution its ramifications transcend national boundaries.'
13. John Richard Thackrah, *Encylopedia of Terrorism and Political Violence* (London and NY: RKP, 1987), p.169.
14. See 'The Task Force Report' in Paul Leventhal and Yohan Alexander, *Preventing Nuclear Terrorism: The Report and Papers of the International Task Force on Prevention of Nuclear Terrorism* (Lexington and Toronto Books 1987), p.7. The three other imperatives are being highlighted as the prevention of nuclear war between the superpowers, the prevention of the further spread of nuclear weapons, and the prevention of catastrophic nuclear accidents.
15. See R. William Mengel, 'The Impact of Nuclear Terrorism on the Military's Role in Society' in Norton and Greenberg (note 2), p.402.
16. Brian Michael Jenkins, *Will Terrorists Go Nuclear?* (Santa Monica, CA: RAND Corp. Paper, No.P-5541. Nov. 1976), p.2. Jenkins, however, regards the acts aimed at causing thousands or tens of thousand of casualties as maybe the least likely.
17. Robert K. Mullen, 'Nuclear Violence' in Leventhal and Alexander (note 14), p.234.
18. See ibid., p.241.
19. Brian Michael Jenkins, 'International Cooperation in Locating and Recovering Stolen Nuclear Materials', *Terrorism. An International Journal* (July/Aug. 1983), p.570. As I will discuss the black market in section 4, I do not want to go into detail at this point. The fact, however, that a nuclear black market and nuclear 'gifts' by states to organizations exist shall be underlined here already.
20. See ibid., p.571.
21. See ibid.
22. See Schelling (note 1), p.88.
23. See Guy R. Sanan, 'A Review of the Main Published Material Regarding the Likelihood of Nuclear Terrorism', Graduation-Paper, Univ. of St Andrews: St Andrews. Feb. 1991; p.12.

24. See Jozef Goldblat *Arms Control Agreements: A Handbook* (London; Taylor & Francis for SIPRI, 1983), pp.236–41.

25. Mengel, p.408 (my own italics).

26. Walter Laqueur, *The Age of Terrorism* (London: Weidenfeld 1987), p.315.

27. Jenkins, *Likelihood of Nuclear Terrorism*, p.5.

28. See Robert K. Mullen, 'Mass Destruction and Terrorism', *Journal of International Affairs* 32/1 (Spring/Summer 1978), p.65. Schelling writes when given the material 'as a bare minimum, six highly skilled individuals possessing exactly the right skills, and very likely a good number of reliable employees to help with the hob' the bomb can be built by terrorists; see Schelling (note 1), p.83.

29. This is to be seen as the message of the most influential essay written by Mason Willrich and Theodore B. Taylor, 'Nuclear Theft: Risks and Safeguards' in Norton and Greenberg (note 2), pp.57–84.

30. The experts thoroughly agreed on the fact that terrorist already had the technical capability to construct chemical and biological (CB) weapons.

31. See Conference Report by Robert L. Beckman, 'International Terrorism: The Nuclear Dimension', *Terrorism. An International Journal* 8/4 (July/Aug. 1986); p.358. See also Jenkins (note 7), p.5.

32. The fission explosive materials needed are either plutonium (^{239}Pu), high-enriched uranium 238 (^{235}U) or uranium 233 (^{233}U). To give the reader some idea of how fission explosives react and what chemical and physical reaction leads to the explosion of a nuclear device, John S. Foster's article about nuclear weapons in the *Encylopedia Americana* is highly recommended. The crucial paragraph of his article is quoted in Willrich and Taylor (note 29), pp.61–3. See also Schelling (note 1), p.82

33. See Schelling (note 1), p.78. Experts agree on the fact that reactor-grade plutonium can be used for making military high-efficiency fission bombs but suggested that the task of separating it would be too difficult for even sophisticated terrorists without governmental or organisational backing; see Beckman (note 31), p.372.

34. Schelling, p.83.

35. Willrich and Taylor (note 29), p.76.

36. See Louis Rene Beres, *Terrorism and Global Security: The Nuclear Threat* (Boulder, CO: Westview Press, 1979), p.45.

37. See ibid., p.46. See the table by Willrich and Taylor (note 29) in the Appendix.

38. See Beckman (note 31), p.367.

39. See ibid.

40. See Task Force Report (note 14), p.16.

41. See ibid., p.15.

42. See Beckman (note 31), p.368.

43. For this particular evidence of threat see Frank Umbach, 'Control and Security of Nuclear Weapons in the Former USSR', *Aussenpolitik* 43/4 (Winter 1992), p.363. Umbach notes that as there was virtually no terrorist situation up until 1991 in the former Soviet Union resembling that in the West, the motive for PAL-security of the tactical nuclear weapons was not applicable.

44. Both the US and Russia are to withdraw and destroy all warheads for nuclear artillery and short-range surface-to-surface missiles (SSM). The seven Lance SSM battalions have been deactivated and 45 launchers eliminated. All naval warheads (less SLBMs) have been withdrawn; about half are to be destroyed. On 17 Oct. 1991 NATO's Nuclear Planning Group approved US plans to withdraw about 50 per cent of air-delivered weapons from Europe. It is estimated that about 700 tactical nuclear bombs would remain. On 2 July 1992 President Bush announced the successful withdrawal of all nuclear artillery shells, Lance SSM warheads and nuclear depth-bombs from Europe, as well as all tactical nuclear weapons from US Navy ships; *The Military Balance 1992–1993* (London: Brassey's for IISS, 1992), p.14.

45. Mullen (note 17), p.236–7.

46. Mullen (note 28), p.66.

47. See Bruce Hoffman, *The Potential Threat to Commercial Nuclear Facilities* (Santa Monica, CA: RAND Corp. Paper, No.P-7450, March 1985),p.3. The sabotage of a

nuclear reactor, according to Jenkins, may result in a mere shutdown or it could spread radioactive fallout the equivalent of many atomic weapons' Jenkins (note 7), p.3.

48. See Michael Flood, 'Nuclear Sabotage' in: Norton and Greenberg (note 2), p.124. See also Konrad Kellen, 'The Potential for Nuclear Terrorism: A Discussion in Leventhal and Alexander (note 14), pp.123–33 (appendix to his article).

49. See Kellen, pp.123–33. These attacks may be classified as 'low-level' sabotage. The literature, however, almost exclusively deals with the 'worst case' scenarios. For incidents of importance in the United States see the RAND Corporation Report by Bruce Hoffman (note 47) which I already have quoted (esp.99.7-12).

50. Compare Gerald L. Pollack, 'Severe Accidents and Terrorist Threats at Nuclear Reactors' in Leventhal and Alexander (note 14), pp.66–77.

51. See Daniel Hirsch, 'The Truck Bomb and Insider Threats to Nuclear Facilities' in ibid., p.207.

52. See ibid., p.208.

53. Ibid., p.210.

54. See ibid., p.209. See also Flood (note 48), p.135. He does not even rule out a 'kamikaze attack although he assesses this as not very probable.

55. See Hirsch (note 55), p.207 and pp.211–15.

56. Ibid., p.213.

57. The Task Force (see note 14) determines reactor sabotage to be the third most serious form of nuclear terrorism behind two options of nuclear explosion; see Leventhal and Alexander, p.12. Hirsch notes that a nuclear reactor contains one thousand times more radioactivity than the Hiroshima bomb and conservative estimates claim that the effects of reactor sabotage might be 'comparably destructive' to that of a crude fission weapon; see Hirsch (note 51), p.216. In the light of the political, economic and social disorder in the former USSR and in Eastern Europe, their nuclear reactors are highly vulnerable to terrorist attacks.

58. See Mullen (note 17), p.242.

59. Ibid.

60. Ibid.

61. See Mullen (note 28), pp.78–83.

62. Ibid.; p.83.

63. See Mullen (note 17), p.245.

64. E.g., Beres and Mullen.

65. Paul Wilkinson, *Terrorism and the Liberal State* (NY: Wiley 1977), p.49.

66. See Jenkins (note 16), p.4.

67. Ibid. A German Red Army Faction-member once pointed out in an interview that with a nuclear weapon terrorists could make the Chancellor or Germany dance on his desk in front of the press and cameras.

68. See Jenkins (note 7), p.6. Jenkins points out that mass killing is unnecessary as long as killing a few suffices for their purposes. In a statistic, published in his 1985 article only 15–20 per cent of all terrorist acts involved fatalities, of which two-thirds only figures one death. Another expert notes that terrorists 'generally seek to influence people rather than to exterminate them'; Beckman (note 31), p.363.

69. Hoffman (note 47), p.4.

70. See ibid.

71. See Peter deLeon *et al*, *The Threat of Nuclear Terrorism: A Reexamination* (Santa Monica, CA: RAND Corp., Note No. N-27096 Jan. 1988), p.4.

72. See Jenkins (note 7), p.10.

73. See deLeon *et al.* (note 71), p.15. Compared Alexander Rossnagel, 'Terrorismus'; in Constanze Eisenbart and Dieter von Ehrenstein, *Nichtverbreitung von Nuklearwaffen. Krise eines Konzepts* (Heidelberg: FEST, 1990), pp.309–10.

74. See Sanan (note 23), p.36–7.

75. See Rossnagel (note 73), pp.310–13. See also deLeon (note 71), pp.10–12.

76. For the precautions companies should take in case of terrorist acts or disaster (mainly

related to the avoidance of economic loss) see Lucy Kellaway and Patrick Harverson, 'When the sky falls', *Financial Times*, 5 March 1993, p.12.

77. See Thackrah (note 13), p.250.

78. In 1978 Mullen wrote: 'On the one hand the possibility of a threat appears too remote to consider that a credible one will occur in the forseeable future. On the other hand, the potential consequences of such a threat are greater than most natural disasters.'; Mullen (note 28), p.88.

79. A different approach is taken by Thomas C. Schelling, 'Thinking About Nuclear Terrorism', *International Security* 7/1(Summer 1982), pp.71–5.

80. Although reports exist that clearly identify the possibility of the Hizbollah being struck by US tactical nuclear weapons in the Bekaa Valley.

81. See Robert S. MacNamara 'Yes, Do Our Best to Return to Nonnuclear World', *International Herald Tribune*, 24 Feb. 1993, p.6

82. See Umbach (note 43). See also Joachim Krause, 'Risks of Nuclear Proliferation Following the 'Dissolution of the Soviet Union', *Aussenpolitik* 43/4 (Winter 1992), pp.352–61.

83. See MacNamara (note 81), p.6.

84. In 1989 Pakistan, South Africa, and Israel were all believed to be nuclear weapon states. Argentina, Brazil, and Taiwan were estimated to have them soon; and the two Koreas, Libya, Iran, and Iraq were also attempting to acquire nuclear technology; see 'Final Report by the Subcommittee on Terrorism', *North Atlantic Assembly Papers*, Brussels, Jan. 1989; p.23.

85. For a brief evaluation of the Non-Proliferation Treaty and its regime in the future see Hans Blix, 'Verification of Nuclear Non-Proliferation: Securing the Future', *IAEA Bulletin* 34/1 (1992), pp.2–5.

86. Muller points out most importantly the fact which is often forgotten when discussing nuclear matters, that every single kind of civil nuclear export is responsible for a further proliferation of nuclear weapons (because of the impulses of motivation and capacity); see Harald Muller, *Energiepolitik, Nuklearexport und die Weiterverbreitung von Kernwaffen* (Frankfurt: Haag + Herchen, 1978) pp.25–9.

87. In 1992 numerous rumours were circulating about weapon links and weapon sales to third-state parties. Reports in newsmagazines, newspapers and other material were dealing with attempts by the Libyans to employ high-rank nuclear engineers, Tadjikistan wanting to sell enriched uranium, other Arab nations trying to recruit scientists from the former Soviet republics, the Iranians trying to recruit scientists as well. However, Iran was reported to have purchased three tactical nuclear weapons from Kazakhstan which both nations denied. Nevertheless reports went on talking about Iran trying to purchase enriched material from France and having acquired a nuclear weapon. Although all these statements were rendered unfounded according to US officials, the German news programme 'Heute' on 4 March 1993 confirmed the assumption that Iran had acquired nuclear weapons (from Kazakhstan). Apart from these severe problems, the question about the huge amount of disposal of nuclear material remain open. The total former Soviet plutonium stockpile is believed to be in excess of 100,000kg and the highly enriched uranium stockpile is estimated to be 500,000kg. There are repeated reports that the nuclear weapons and the material is being guarded safely; yet, the safety of the material and the security of the weapon arsenals will become a major problem if public order in Russia declines further. According to a 19 March 1993 British Channel 4 TV report, 100kg of uranium were missing from a Siberian factory. Russian allegations, on the other hand, point out that Ukraine is unable to guarantee the safety of the nuclear weapons located on its territory; see Chrystia Freeland, 'Ukraine says nuclear fears are unfounded', *Financial Times*, 5 March 1993, p.3. For the information above see *Interim Report by the Sub-Committee on Verification and Technology*; Scientific and Technical Committee, North Atlantic Assembly: Brussels, Nov. 1992; pp.3–9 and Krause, (note 82), pp.356–9.

88. See *Interim Report*; pp.6–7. Krause points out that '[b]etween 2000 and 3000 [people] rank as specialists for the construction of nuclear weapons. Many of these specialists could be interesting contacts for Third World states with nuclear ambitions in the military field but with too few experts of this own'; Krause (note 82), p.359.

89. According to the RAND Note by deLeon *et al.* (note 71), p.9, the worldwide commercial nuclear power industry could move to a plutonium-based fuel cycle within the next decade or two.

90. Two German companies NTG and PTB exported from 1983 through to 1988 nuclear-technical machines, components and fissile material without any export-license to India and to Pakistan; see Alexander Rossnagel, 'Schwarzmarkt' in Eisenbart and Ehrenstein (note 73), p.316.

91. The Sudan, e.g., from 1980–87 was one of the leading illegal trading-places for high-grade nuclear weapons material; see ibid.

92. See Herbert Dixon, 'Physical Security of Nuclear Facilities' in Leventhal and Alexander (note 14), pp.191–206.

93. It is Rossnagel's belief that the more effective the review, defense and safety measures are, the stronger they cut into the citizen's liberty; see Rossnagel, 'Objektschutz',in Eisenbart and Ehrenstein (note 73), p.353.

94. See ibid., p.354.

95. *IHT*, 5 March 1993; p.3.

96. See Sidney Moglewer, 'International Safeguards and Nuclear Terrorism'; in Leventhal and Alexander (note 14), p.249.

97. See ibid., p.252.

98. For improvement measures on behalf of the effectiveness of the IAEA see J. Jennekens, R. Parsick, and A von Baeckmann, 'Strengthening the international safeguard system;, *IAEA Bulletin* 34/1 (1992), pp.6–10.

99. Terrorists either produce the chemicals themselves or they obtain them by theft. E.g., in 1975 the Red Army Faction in West Germany stole 53 steel bottles containing mustard gas; see Neil C. Livingstone, *The War against Terrorism* (Lexington and Toronto: Lexington Books, 1982), p.11.

100. See Mullen (note 28), p.76–7.

101. See ibid., p.77. A potentially dangerous threat that should not be underestimated is sabotage by terrorist of chemical plants, railway tank cars carrying dangerous chemicals or change of labels on dangerous chemicals stored in sacks or drums; see Livingstone (note 99), p.114.

102. See *The Rio Summit and the Chemical Warfare Convention* (Brussels: Scientific and Technical Committee, North Atlantic Assembly, Nov. 1992), pp.13–17.

103. See Mullen (note 28), p.78.

104. Ibid. (my own italics)

105. See Livingstone (note 99), p.114.

106. Mullen, p.78.

107. Although the Non-Proliferation Treaty in 1968 was designed to bring proliferation of nuclear weapons to a halt, the 'nuclear club' has nevertheless extended to an amount of about 13 (potential) nuclear weapon states by 1993.

108. So predicted by Jenkins; see Brian M. Jenkins, 'The Future Course of International Terrorism' in Wilkinson, *Contemporary Research on Terrorism*, p.588.

109. This insecurity is being exploited by terrorists using the means of nuclear hoaxes.

Application of Technology to Aviation Security

RODNEY WALLIS

This paper suggests that the air transport industry may have failed to maximize the security benefits available through 'high-tech' developments despite its dependence on technological advances in all other areas of its operations. It highlights passenger and baggage reconciliation as the 'bedrock of any defence against the baggage bomber' and cites the introduction of computer-based, automated matching programmes at Frankfurt's International Airport to demonstrate their feasible application at major gateways. Consideration is given in the text to the role and viability of the X-ray as a security tool; warns against 'cosmetic' security; touches upon vapour analysis techniques as a means to detect improvised explosive devices and discusses computer-based access controls. Despite the various technological advances, the paper suggests the human element will remain a key ingredient in the aviation security mix.

In my various papers published during the 11 years I was Director of Security at the International Air Transport Association (IATA), I gave clear indication of my belief in a systems approach to aviation security. There is no 'silver bullet' to use against the terrorist: thus a building block approach to maximise our defences is essential. This paper is just one aspect of aviation security and is presented in that context.

In many respects, the application of technology to aviation security can be considered a story of missed opportunities. Yet, Civil Aviation, of all the service industries, must be perceived as the most technologically minded. From the supersonic Concorde spearheading a multi-billion pound investment in aircraft to the multifarious computer systems developed to handle passenger acceptance processes or to deal with the complex accounting systems, 'high-tech' dominates thinking in the world of civil aviation. The industry depends on state-of-the-art equipment to move people and their baggage through the major international airports. Similar equipment is a necessity to account for passengers purchases of tickets and to transfer money between airlines and travel agents and from one country to another. Such technology helps simplify processes which make it possible for a passenger to buy a ticket in one country for travel to and through many others and on several different airlines. Here is technology being applied to the commercial world of air transportation.

None of it would be possible without the application of technology to all facets of airline and airport operations. Given such obvious and visible evolution, it would be instructive to conclude that similar technological development has been applied to the security of aircraft and airports and to the passengers and crew. It would also be natural for the general public to assume that just as pilots and accounting staff are professionally trained to maximise the benefits of the new age technology, so too are the personnel appointed to provide security services to the international air companies and to airports. Regrettably, any such assumption on a global basis would be incorrect.

High-tech is applied to aircraft to make them fly faster and further carrying ever larger payloads. The driving force is profitability. The effect of improved performance is easy both to measure and to comprehend. Without the application of state-of-the-art computers and their associated equipment, passengers could not be booked or handled at airports in sufficient numbers to capitalise on the improvements in aircraft. The cost effectiveness of any investment in the area of aircraft and passenger operations can be measured and, of course, there is no alternative to such investment.

It is very different when it comes to provision of security services. Not all airlines relate the furnishing of security services to the effective management of their operations. The impression which some have is that security, just like immigration and customs, is a hindrance to the smooth flow of passengers through an airport and onto an aircraft and thus a debit rather than a credit to their business. Security regulations are seen by many to be unnecessary annoyances. Some live ostrich-like with their heads in the sand believing that terrorism will pass them by.

In June 1992 a federal court in New York hearing charges of wilful misconduct being brought against Pan American in respect of the Lockerbie tragedy, learned that the Federal Aviation Administration mandated security rules were abandoned by Pan American because they were 'time consuming and a very difficult venture'. Pan American was an airline of the developed world and registered in a country where a committed administration not only identified risks facing their carriers but also regulated for the protection of the passengers. It is a fact that technology, both high-tech and low-tech, existed at the time of the Lockerbie disaster (December 1988) which in one case would have eliminated and in the other reduced the 'time consuming' and 'difficult' elements of the abandoned procedure. The procedure was 'positive passenger baggage match'. The lives of 270 people could have been protected by the application of technology. It must be noted that the Boeing 747 jumbo jet was destroyed through the terrorists' use of technology.

Pan American failed to apply all available technology to their security programme, but it has to be noted that the governments with security responsibility for airport operations at London and Frankfurt had not mandated the use of passenger/baggage match for interline baggage. The International Civil Aviation Organization (ICAO), as a United Nations Agency, did not require the procedure until April 1989. It is a sad fact that even today, although the United Kingdom was among the first governments to acknowledge ICAO's international standards for security and indeed helped write them, the UK has still to call for the full implementation of passenger baggage matching.

Three months before Lockerbie, the European Civil Aviation Conference (ECAC), comprising at that time the 25 states of Western Europe, published the third edition of their 'Manual of ECAC Recommendations and Resolutions relating to Facilitation and Security Matters'. One section of the manual contains 'Guiding Principles on Automated Systems for the Identification of Checked-in Baggage'. Recognising the need to automate reconciliation procedures at the major airports and, in effect, calling for technology to be harnessed to the security programme, one ECAC 'essential element' of the Guidelines called for the:

> Introduction of records in the automated Departure Control System at airports which should contain the coded reference numbers allocated to passengers and their baggage, as well as baggage locations in aircraft holds which, eventually, should identify the reference numbers of all baggage loaded with those of the passengers having boarded the aircraft.

ECAC in 1988 had gone further than ICAO. ICAO amended their standard in 1989 to come much closer to the ECAC and the International Air Transport Association (IATA) ideal. This reflected the airline industry's own recommendations.

Following the destruction of Air India's Boeing 747 in June 1985, the international airlines were called to a special meeting of IATA's Security Advisory Committee in Montreal. Debate made it clear that a passenger and the passenger's baggage had to be considered a single entity. A technical working group was established to develop procedures and specifications to enable this to be done. We had to protect against a bag travelling on its own and unauthorised on aircraft. By July 1987 the work was complete and had received universal acceptance by the airlines. ICAO adopted the time-scale identified as practicable by the airlines, namely that by April 1989, the entire industry could have in place a fully automated system of passenger/baggage reconciliation, compatible with manual systems, for use with interline baggage. It would identify the rogue bag. With ICAO's adoption came the plea that government should, where possible, push ahead of the agreed applicability date. Indeed for point-to-point baggage they were mandated to do so by December 1987.

It is good to know that after a slow start, the German partners in civil aviation security have come together to develop and introduce a fully automated passenger/baggage, baggage/passenger reconciliation system. This meets fully the intent of ICAO and ECAC. The FAG (the airport authority at Frankfurt) together with Lufthansa, the computer giant IBM and a local software company, have in place in Frankfurt Airport's Terminal A (used by Lufthansa) a system based on IATA's resolutions and recommended practices. Frankfurt has the tightest 'minimum connecting times' for inter-line operations in Europe. The new system allows the airport to maintain the integrity of the inter-line element of their traffic. It will be extended to the remaining terminals following its initial introduction. The FAG will manage the programme for all carriers. Ultimately, it will be possible to drive the baggage sorting system itself by the bar codes encrypted onto the baggage tags. This is a far cry from the former UK Minister of Civil Aviation Lord Brabazon's claim in a letter to the British media that reconciliation–the bedrock of any defence against the baggage bomber, a description given to the procedure by the US President's Commission on Terrorism–would close an airport down. The former minister's position may explain, or perhaps reflect, his department's disinclination to support developments in the UK which are similar in concept to the one now emerging in Germany.

In a different area of security, there is a very real danger of the misapplication of technology. Within Europe, the United Kingdom's Department of Transport is calling for the 100 per cent screening of all checked baggage. With today's technology, that means x-ray screening. The Air Transport Industry knows very well the inability of x-rays to detect modern improvised explosive devices. ICAO established a diplomatic conference leading to the adoption of a Convention for the Marking of Plastic Explosives for the very reason that neither x-ray nor explosive vapour detection was a reliable means to identify the presence of explosive materials in baggage. On this point, I would suggest that the success of the Convention lies well into the future for there is sufficient unmarked Semtex, quite apart from other, similar and easily manufactured material, already in existence to last your lifetime and mine and those of our children too. It is good to dot legislative 'i's' but as a defence against the saboteur, the new Convention is unlikely to prove a panacea.

Europe has not adopted the UK approach for the 100 per cent screening of checked baggage. They have set the year 2000 as a target date for such a standard. By that time, it was hoped that technology would have caught up with the needs of civil aviation. If not, the target will be reviewed. In the meantime, 100 per cent screening of checked baggage is a very dangerous concept for government administrations to press into premature service. We all know that routine leads to familiarity which in turn breeds contempt. Using an x-ray to interrogate an already suspect bag makes sense if it is just part of a secondary screening process (one of the security building bricks), Thus 100 per cent screening would be mis-using technology simply to provide an artificial appearance for security operations. It will aid and abet the terrorist rather than deter them. Terrorists know all about the technology available to the industry. The task of the security specialist is to convince these criminals that our use of it offers maximum protection to the airline.

The newly appointed Director General of the Airports Associations Council International (AACI), Oris Dunham, has recently spoken on this very subject. He said in an interview published in June 1992 that the 'AACI is fundamentally opposed to cosmetic security measures designed to allay public concern rather than to reduce the risks of unlawful interference.'

Despite this, one airport authority, has given indications of supporting 100 per cent x-ray examination of checked baggage. The motivation is twofold. First to 'allay public concern'. That is the cosmetic approach. The second reason, and more important from the authority's viewpoint, is to move people more quickly through security controls freeing them to spend more time among the ever growing conglomeration of shopping facilities which provide a very healthy input to airport revenues. Technology is being applied for reasons other than the protection of the travelling public.

The two most discussed terrorist incidents involving large aircraft used improvised explosive devices to bring the aircraft down. Air India in 1985 was ruled to have been attacked by a radio bomb carried in an unaccompanied suitcase. In July 1992 the Indian authorities arrested a member of a Sikh terrorist group on grounds of his complicity in the crime. Pan American 103 in 1988 was destroyed by a similar technique. This time indictments have been issued by the Scottish and US authorities against two Libyans – both with airline connections. There have been other similar attacks. Union de Transports Aeriens (UTA), Korean Air, Trans World Airlines have each suffered from the technological ability of the terrorists' bomb makers. What has been the industry's response?

An immediate reaction by Transport Canada to the Air India bombing was the introduction of x-ray machines for use in connection with all international flights. It was a natural and instinctive reaction but it was short-lived. The Canadians quickly concluded that x-ray technology in 1985 was insufficiently advanced to identify modern improvised explosive devices. The policy was abandoned. Quite correctly so. The Canadians threw their full weight behind passenger and baggage reconciliation. They initiated action in ICAO. The FAA in reviewing the environment in which their carriers were operating at that time introduced major amendments to the Air Carrier Standard Security Programme (ACSSP). They avoided dependence on x-ray technology. In section 15C 1(a) of the ACSSP, the American authorities called for positive passenger baggage matching to identify any unaccompanied bags. Such bags then had to be physically searched or not carried. There was no role for the x-ray nor indeed for vapour analysis. That very excellent rule stands today. It was just that regulation which a federal jury in New York noted Pan American elected to abandon in 1988. The questionable value of the x-ray in relation to checked baggage was raised by the US President's Commission on Terrorism and by the Scottish Sheriff Principal in his Determination in the Fatal Accident Inquiry into the Lockerbie tragedy. It is also reflected in the German decision to press ahead with a fully automated reconciliation system which rejects any reliance on the x-ray machine.

Since 1985 there have been major improvements in x-ray technology. Colour enhanced imaging can now identify between organic and inorganic materials and automatic imaging has been developed but the machines still cannot tell you if plastic explosive is being carried as distinct from harmless plastic containers or toys, and this assumes the explosive material is not hidden. Prior to Lockerbie, the German police had warned that the bombs found in their raids on certain terrorists' properties would be very hard to identify by conventional screening methods. Since vast quantities of plastic material is carried by passengers on today's aircraft, the value of dual energy systems must be debated. The role of the x-ray in 1992 is no more, or less significant than it was in 1985 – it is simply a tool to help security screeners determine whether a bag is carrying questionable objects. That requires effective training of the staff. Given the infrequency of bombs being carried on board aircraft in checked baggage – Air India in 1985, Pan Am in 1988 and UTA in 1989 – and the billion and a half checked bags carried every

year, the potential for discovery by routine, conventional x-ray examination is very slim indeed. Aviation's defence against the baggage
bomber must not be dependent on the use of this technology.

Notwithstanding criticism of x-rays as a means to detect the type of
bomb which destroyed Pan Am 103, there is, of course, a role for x-ray
screening as a support mechanism for properly trained security staff.
Principally this is in the area of hand baggage screening. When the FAA
introduced their monitoring programme for screening personnel in 1987,
the administration's inspectors, using test weapons, were able to avoid
detection on 20 per cent of the occasions they checked the security performance. One evasion could have been disastrous had the person
involved been a terrorist. The FAA monitoring, coupled with a system
of imposed fines ($2 million in the first two sweeps), has ensured that
standards have significantly improved since 1987. However, x-ray technology applied in the search of guns and knives in hand baggage is
different to seeking to discover the terrorists' 1980s weapon, the improvised explosive device placed in the suitcase.

X-rays could have a role to play in respect of cargo security. To date,
very little has been done to protect civil aviation against the potential
use by terrorists of cargo shipments as a means to get a bomb on an aircraft. Some governments require cargo shipments to be delayed 24
hours. For what purpose? Have they not heard of the technological
advances which have given us the digital watch and timer? The drug
barons of South America have shown how easy it is to move narcotics
illicitly among cargo shipments. If cocaine can travel that way so too can
Semtex.

The value of x-ray technology for the examination of cargo is that it
can be used in conjunction with an air waybill. The air waybill details the
contents of a consignment – the x-ray may be able to confirm the legiti-
macy of the contents. I submitted papers in 1989 and 1991 on behalf of
IATA to the ICAO seeking standards to be set for cargo security and
for these to be incorporated into Annex 17 to the Chicago Convention
on International Civil Aviation. A working group comprising the USA
(FAA), the UK (Dept. of Transport) and IATA (myself) put up a joint
paper in 1990. Provisional acceptance of my 1991 proposals has been
given but to date no further action has been taken. We are losing an
opportunity to be pre-emptive. The political scenario which has given us
stability in respect of airborne terrorism over the past three years may
not hold forever. We should not have to wait for an incident before we
put our house in order.

Advances in x-ray technology are continuing. These include the
ability to super-impose onto the screener's visual display unit (VDU)

images of weapons which the staff member should identify. Staff performance can be tested without the use of test weapons. Any procedure to maintain the attentions of screening staff is welcome. X-ray technology, linked to computer analysis of the images and utilising atomic weights to help identify contents of bags is moving the industry in the right direction but at a cost. Whether airlines will consider the cost justified remains debatable. In any event, if we are to utilise 'state-of-the-art' machinery, it is vital that the operators be trained to maximise the potential. The two go hand in hand until such time as automatic imaging can be linked to recognition. Even then someone will have to respond to alarm.

The need in civil aviation remains the upgrading of the recruitment, selection, training and management of security staff. This is essential if we are to maximise the benefits brought about by improvements in the technical equipment. The human element remains the number one ingredient in a security programme. I can only repeat an earlier warning of mine that 'it is no use having high-tech equipment if we use low-tech people to operate it.'

Metal detectors, whether fixed position items such as the walk-through magnetometers or mobile, handheld wands have been a real deterrent to those persons wanting to secrete weapons on their persons when walking through security screening points. They are not a barrier to professional terrorists as we have seen in past incidents. The April 1988 seizure of the Kuwait Airways 747 en route from Bangkok to that Gulf state was accomplished regardless of the fact that magnetometers (and x-rays) existed in Bangkok's Don Muang Airport. The simple fact was that on that occasion, passengers have attested to the fact that no attention was paid either to the warning alarms of the magnetometer or the images which appeared on the VDU screen. Passengers on board the seized aircraft and whom I was able to debrief in London, confirmed that no one was monitoring the VDU and, while alarms were initiated when they walked through the metal detector arches, no one attempted to check the reasons. Technological aids may be present at airports but unless they are effectively used, application of modern equipment is quite useless.

Another area of technology which in principle provides civil aviation with a support tool to meet the security standards developed by ICAO is mass spectrometry. Various forms of vapour detectors have been developed and tested. A Canadian product was available and in use in 1985 at Toronto when the bags carrying the improvised explosive devices were checked in for their journeys on Canadian Pacific for trans-shipment to Air India. The bombs were not detected. Technological advances have refined the techniques available in 1985 and equipment exists which varies from British Aerospace's Condor with, initially a seven-figure price tag, to the latest Canadian portable sniffer which can be contained in a brief case. Such products are easier to obtain than a good dog team but some would still indicate their preference for canines providing the handler is as intelligent as the dog – not necessarily always the case.

The problem facing any form of vapour detection is the low vapour threshold of modern plastic explosives. This subject featured in an earlier civil litigation in New York, this time involving TWA who were the victims of an under-seat bomb which killed four passengers on a flight from Rome to Athens in 1986. X-ray examination had failed to identify the improvised explosive device and the prosecution honed in on the fact that no attempt was made to use trained sniffer dogs to identify the presence of plastic explosive. On this occasion too the jury found for the plaintiffs. It is difficult to know how much weight the jurors would have placed on the international opinion developed subsequently within ICAO had that viewpoint been available at the time of the litigation.

The air transport industry must maximise the benefits of technology applied to civil aviation security operations. This requires linking 'state-of-the-art' equipment to properly selected, trained and motivated staff. Responsibility to ensure that this happens rests with governments.

In another area of research and development into high-tech defences against the saboteur, and working with the benefit of an FAA contract, a Californian research company developed a Thermal Neutron Activation process (TNA) which sought to improve on existing detection technology. The system met with strong opposition from US-based carriers from the very beginning. It was noted without too much enthusiasm by other international carriers. The lack of support was claimed to be on the basis of the weight of the machine (airport floors would not carry the ten tons), the slowness of the process (a maximum throughput of 400 bags an hour), its reject rate (5 per cent), its acceptability from a safety viewpoint (the system is based on nuclear process) and, as always in aviation its cost. The first estimates suggested each machine would require an outlay of $750,000.

All the points raised in objection to TNA were valid but it was a step forward and the carriers should have supported the research being undertaken. Only by pushing new techniques will effective technological defences be developed for use against the terrorists. The cost of the TNA research was coming from the federal pocket rather than from the airlines directly. In the aftermath of Lockerbie, the US President's

Commission on Terrorism centred one of its criticisms on the decision to push ahead with TNA – it was too much, too soon. The FAA subsequently dropped the requirement.

Technology does seem to offer better opportunities for success when it comes to access control. Computer-issued identification cards and controlled doors linked to a central data bank is one aspect where technology can be and is applied today to protect sensitive areas of airports. This does have the potential of an Orwellian scenario with 'big brother' watching over the workforce, but if it improves security it is a small price to pay. At present there are obvious loopholes but ultimately the use of fingerprints or palm-prints to give access through controlled points will be possible. This will eliminate the possibility of cards being borrowed for illicit use. I notice that the US Immigration Service is already experimenting with just such a system.

Following the FAA's proposed introduction of computer-based access control systems, the airports in the United States led the opposition to the proposal. In this respect, I was very interested to read in the August 1992 *Jane's Airport Review*, an article detailing an interview with the FAA's Director, Office of Civil Aviation Security Policy and Planning. He indicated that the administration is rolling back the scheme, which should make it more acceptable to the operators, and that the administration was seeking a partnership with the operators in developing new security standards. As most of you know very well, partnership of the entities involved in civil aviation security is a gospel I preached throughout all of the last decade. I do so today. The airlines and the control authorities were able to work in harness in the fight against the illegal carriage of narcotics on civil aircraft and in areas of immigration control. There is every reason to believe airlines, airports and civil aviation authorities could pull as a team in security matters but it will take changes on all sides for this to happen.

ICAO has not legislated on computer-based access controls and given the mix of nations who make up the UN Agency, it is unlikely that they will for a long time to come. The wealthier nations with greater exposure to terrorism and more complex airports to guard do not have to wait for ICAO to deliberate before introducing security measures.

Automation utilising the latest and best equipment is not an absolute requirement for safeguarding civil aviation. Resorting to high-tech solutions at airports the size of Amsterdam, London or New York is necessitated by their size and complexity. Levels of labour costs is another vital factor. In locations where the workforce is less expensive and where there are only a comparatively few departures each day, manual approaches are just as effective as their automated counterparts and in some cases more so. In such cases, technology is best left on the manu-facturer's shelf. It is financially beyond the reach of the developing world; it is not necessary; it will invariably be ill-used; it will not help safeguard the travelling public!

Whatever system of access control is used – technology based in the west, labour based in the developing world – in situations where there is visual or machine matching of the card with its owner, it is essential that those responsible for the process are adequately monitored to ensure compliance with the rules. At Karachi in 1986 the attack on the Pan American aircraft could have been prevented, or at least delayed, if the gate guards had stopped the vehicle carrying the terrorists and sought to examine their badges. Doubtless the perpetrators were well aware of the practice of simply waving vehicles through with not even a casual glance at the identification cards. Similar scenes can be witnessed in the developed countries, especially on rainy days at motor access points! Guards prefer the warmth of a dry cabin rather than the discomfort of standing in the wet to check identifications.

Intrusion detection devices using variations of broken beam tech-nology can be used to protect aircraft but use of manpower is a legitimate alternative. The ability to lock an aircraft door would also help protect aircraft from unlawful entry. Technology correctly applied is one way but the use of people working in a non-industrial environ-ment can match the best that high-tech has to offer.

Summing up, I would suggest that technology applied to civil aviation security had certain successes in the early 1970s against the embryo ter-rorist. The technology was simple and easily applied by the industry. Today's airport scene continues to reflect developments from that period. In the present economic environment, airline and airport managements will only voluntarily adopt systems which can be shown to have facilitation, operational or marketing benefits If they are simply to provide security measures, there is a danger that many of the companies will require encouragement from the authorities before they are im-plemented. For example, FAA had to impose fines on US airlines before the carriers raised the levels of security at hand baggage screen-ing points.

If governments develop their regulations in partnership with the oper-ators, and that does not mean subordinating national interests to commercial ones, airlines and airports will more easily understand and accept their responsibilities. At that time we can expect to see greater and more effective use of the technological advances likely to become available to protect the users of air transportation. It is a challenge for the balance of the 1990s.

Explosive Detection for Commercial Aircraft Security

The destruction of Pan Am Flight 103 in December 1988 over Lockerbie in Scotland captured the attention of the world and highlighted the vulnerability of commercial aircraft to determined terrorists using sophisticated explosives technology. It is clearly important to find the means to diminish this vulnerability. As part of this effort, it is essential to develop and improve the capability to detect plastic explosive materials of the type used against Flight 103. Any technology for explosive detection will of course be embedded in a complex operational environment that might be penetrated by avoiding the path where detection could occur, or by failure of those charged with employing the technology to exploit fully its information content. Thus, although no combination of technologies could be expected to provide complete protection against the wide range of possible threats, it should be possible to improve the odds appreciably by increasing the probability that any particular explosive will be detected.

A. The Threat Environment

The primary threat of concern to aviation over the past two decades has been weapons in the hands of hijackers. Currently x-ray machines are used for searching hand luggage and metal detectors are used for searching passengers. These devices are widely used at airports throughout the world and they have been impressively effective at detecting such weapons and deterring potential hijackers. The searches are non-intrusive and present only a slight inconvenience and occasional delay which the travelling public has been willing to accept. However, more sophisticated devices such as plastic explosives are not readily detectable by either the metal detectors or the standard x-ray devices. Explosives devices fabricated from these materials can be carried by a suicidal terrorist, an unwitting passenger, or checked with luggage by equipping the explosives with a detonation system that has a time delay or is altimeter controlled.

There is a variety of ways that explosives might be brought onto aircraft. Some of these are illustrated in Figure 1. Although most of this

FIGURE 1
AIRCRAFT ACCESS

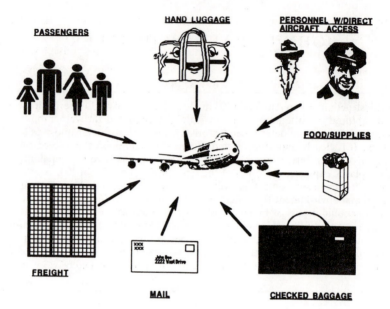

TABLE 1
THE THREAT ENVIRONMENT

7 Million	Aircraft Departures/year from US Airports
500 Million	Passengers/year departing from US Airports
1 Billion	Bags/year departing from US Airports
17	High-threat US Airports
45	High-threat Foreign Airports

Peak Loads for 1 Airline at JFK in a 3-hour period

19	International Flights
6,000	Passengers
12,000	Bags = 4000 Bags/Hr. or 70 Bags/Min.

~1	Explosive Incident/year on US carriers

report will be concerned with explosives carried by personnel or in-hand or checked luggage, other routes clearly represent major vulnerabilities.

Any detection system must also be designed to cope with the magnitude of the problem. Some of the dimensions of the threat environment are described in Table 1. Based on the historical number of incidents on board US air carriers, the explosive detection system must have a significant probability of detecting one explosive device per year while searching over 500 million passengers, and roughly one billion items of luggage per year. An additional complication is that the search must cope with substantial peak loads as also illustrated in Table 1.

The types of explosives that represent the most probable threat are listed in Table 1. It is important to note that common explosives are typically not pure materials and very often contain in addition to several different types of explosives, contaminants, binders, solvent residues, and impurities.

The chemical structures of some of these materials are given in detail in Figure 2. It is evident that these commonly used high explosives contain many atoms of nitrogen in addition to carbon, oxygen, and hydrogen. However, not all high explosives contain nitrogen suggesting that a comprehensive search strategy must include devices whose detection capability is not dependent on the presence of nitrogen atoms. A

TABLE 2

TYPES OF EXPLOSIVES

HIGH THREAT	LOW THREAT
RDX	TNT
HMX	Dynamite
PETN	Nitroglycerine
C-4	Nitrocellulose
DATASHEET	Hydrogels
SEMTEX	NH_4NO_3

Contaminants / Binders / Solvent Residues / Impurities

OTHER THREATS

Toxic Chemicals, etc.

FIGURE 2

CHEMICAL STRUCTURES OF SEVERAL COMMON EXPLOSIVES

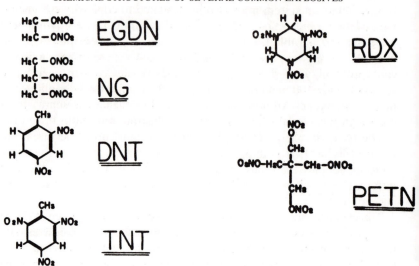

FIGURE 3

CONCEALED SEMTEX BOMB

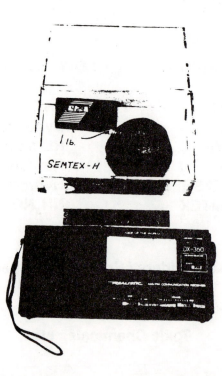

full device of course includes in addition to the explosive component, a detonator, timer or altimeter, batteries, and wiring all of which provide threat signatures. The nature of threats vary from crude devices such as a pipe bomb, or sticks of dynamite with an alarm clock to sophisticated weapons incorporating sheet explosive (deta sheet) integrated into the walls of a suitcase and explosives packed into an electronic device to conceal the detonator, timer, wiring and battery.

Figure 3 illustrates a lump of plastic explosive, detonator, and timer that could be easily concealed in an electronic device. It is important to understand that a detection device may still make a useful contribution to deterrence even though it is not capable of handling the entire range of possible threats.

B. Statistics of Detection Decisions

The performance of a detection system is limited by two kinds of potential errors: an error of omission (a false negative) characterised by failing to detect a true threat, and an error of commission (a false positive) whereby a non-threatening object is judged to be one that does pose a threat. Many aspects of decision-making involve the problem of detection with a potential error. The formal terms typically used for these errors as well as for their complements are displayed in Table 3 where the rows represent the presence or absence of the threat, and the

TABLE 3

DETECTION DECISIONS

DETECTION DECISION

		YES	NO
ACTUAL THREAT	YES	TRUE POSITIVE (SENSITIVITY)	FALSE NEGATIVE
	NO	FALSE POSITIVE	TRUE NEGATIVE (SPECIFICITY)

columns are the result of the screen that either raises the alarm or fails to do so. The performance of detection systems is often described in terms of the probability of detection (true positive probability) and the probability of false alarm (the false positive probability). The impact of an error of omission, or an error of commission is quite different. If one terrorist action per year in bringing an explosive onto an airplane is anticipated, then with a 95 per cent probability of detection, only infrequently will a terrorist manage to get through the system and destroy the airplane. However, the impact of such a loss can be catastrophic. On the other hand, a 5 per cent false alarm rate is less dramatic but much more persistent. For a 400-passenger aircraft, assuming an average of two bags per passenger, approximately 40 of the bags would trigger an alarm. The false alarm requires some form of response, most likely a more careful screening to determine that it is not a threat.

Given the large volume of luggage and passengers that must be dealt with, and considering the extremely low probability of a true positive in any search, a succession of screening stages would appear to be warranted. These would range from an inexpensive and high throughput initial screen (with high probability of detection) to a thorough examination for the most suspicious cases. This basic strategy involves passing most of the bags through a very efficient low-cost screen with low delay or disruption, and then selecting the smaller number that fail the screen for more careful and thorough scrutiny involving greater time and more sophisticated – and presumably more expensive – means of detection. By this means, the flow rate through the expensive, slow, more elaborate screens is kept to a reasonable level, limiting the number of such instruments that have to be purchased and the number of passengers who suffer the associated delay.

For any given technology, the probability of detection (PD) and the probability of false alarm (PFA) are linked through the selection of a detection threshold, as illustrated in Figure 4. If the threshold is set to a low value of the detection parameter, many non-explosive containing bags will trigger an alarm; in this case the PFA will be high, but the PD will also be high, so it is less likely that a true explosive will be missed. On the other hand, if the threshold is set high, the PFA is reduced, but there is a greater risk that a true explosive will not be detected. It is thus necessary to have reasonably good estimates of the PD, and PFA associated with any particular detection instrument under varying operational conditions to assess the associated consequences. Then, a trade-off will have to be made between risk of failing to detect an explosive (clearly an issue of low frequency, but very high consequences), and the frequency which false alarms are triggered so that passengers and airlines must suffer the cost and disruption associated with delays and searches (an issue of daily concern).

C. Technologies for Explosive Detection

Many approaches have been considered for the purpose of detecting explosives that have been secreted in containers or suitcases, or are carried on personnel. These methods can be divided into those that rely on bulk properties of the explosive device, and those which rely on detecting explosive signatures in the vapour phase. Most of the methods that rely on bulk properties use nuclear, x-ray, or magnetic resonance techniques.

Nuclear Methods

Nuclear methods for explosive detection involve some means of exciting or activating the nuclei of atoms in an explosive in such a way that they emit radiation that is characteristic of the elements involved. This radiation is then observed using a suitable detector. Usually these measurements are carried out under ideal laboratory conditions. Unfortunately, in an airport environment, and in the time available for inspection, the conditions are far from ideal for applying these methods to the detection of explosives inside a suitcase filled with many kinds of materials. However, nuclear methods have been developed that make it

FIGURE 4

FREQUENCY DISTRIBUTIONS

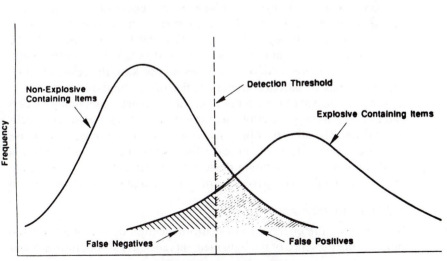

possible to detect nitrogen and other atoms characteristic of explosives such as oxygen and carbon.

To use a nuclear method the nucleus of an atom must be excited by some form of penetrating radiation that can pass through the luggage material as well as through the explosive. Typically, only neutrons or gamma rays are suitable. Similarly, the characteristic radiation produced by nucleii in the explosive must be able to escape from the luggage so that again the radiation is typically limited to neutrons or gamma rays.

1. Thermal Neutron Activation

With the thermal neutron activation (TNA) detection method, the luggage to be examined is moved into a radiation-shielded chamber in which it is bombarded with thermal (low energy) neutrons. The thermal neutrons can be captured by nuclei of the elements in the materials comprising the luggage and its contents. Neutron capture by one of these nuclei results in a new neuclues, one neutron heavier, which then most commonly emits one or more gamma rays. A suitable arrangement of multiple-gamma detectors records and identifies these gamma rays and also provides a crude location of their origin within the luggage through appropriate computer analysis of the multiple-detector data. Fortunately, the characteristic gamma ray emitted by nitrogen is of considerably higher energy than those given off by other nuclei that make up the typical materials found in suitcases. Thus the major component nitrogen, that characterises the most common military and industrial explosives can be detected in a relatively straightforward fashion. Computer analysis then locates any region of dense nitrogen-containing material that could be identified as an explosive.

Of course, any nitrogen-containing material in a suitcase will give basically the same gamma-ray signature as do explosives. Fortunately, most common items carried in suitcases do not have the relatively high concentrations of nitrogen characteristics of plastic explosives. Nonetheless, the chance of benign but detectable nitrogen containing objects makes it imperative to complement this method with one that will delineate more accurately the object under scrutiny. It is also possible to use TNA extremely effectively in specialised ways. For example, TNA is ideal for screening electronic devices which should have a negligible nitrogen content in comparison with even a small explosive device.

2. Elastic Neutron Scattering

By measuring the energy loss of neutrons scattered from objects in the suitcase, the presence of the light elements such as carbon, nitrogen and oxygen contained in explosives can be detected specifically and also measured quantitatively. The low atomic weight elements present in plastic explosives can be relatively easily differentiated from materials composed of higher atomic weight elements. The most significant problem with this technique is the presence of background neutrons. How much background can be tolerated in terms of multiple-scattered elastic neutrons from the luggage and from the associated shielding and other luggage-handling components surrounding the luggage is yet to be determined. An explosive detection device based on this technology would also require a moderately sophisticated accelerator to generate the neutron beam. The operation of such a device in an airport environment remains a significant challenge.

3. Pulsed Fast Neutron Activation (PFNA)

With the Pulsed Fast Neutron Activation (PFNA) method, luggage is bombarded by high energy neutrons, usually provided by an accelerator. These fast neutrons are extremely penetrating and could easily pass through the luggage several times; in fact they could be used to penetrate a whole cargo carrier of luggage. Instead of being captured as in the thermal neutron case, the fast neutrons activate the nuclei by inelastic scattering. The de-excitation of these nuclei results in the emission of generally low energy gamma rays that are characteristic of the nuclear species. In the case of explosives, the gamma rays are produced by the activation of the nuclei of nitrogen, oxygen and carbon. In principle, PFNA can provide not only identification of these three main components of explosives but also measure their relative abundance. The measured nitrogen-oxygen-carbon ratios can then be compared with those known to exist in explosives. In principle, PFNA might provide a 'chemical analysis' of the nitrogen-containing materials of interest. By using a pulsed neutron source it is possible to measure the gamma rays produced as a function of the time of flight of the neutrons through the target. The neutron time of flight is used to provide information on the location of a detected element in a target by correlating the measured time of the event with the gamma rays that are produced.

As noted above, the background problem with fast neutrons is much more severe than that experienced with thermal neutrons and the design of an appropriate detector geometry for the interrogation of luggage is not a simple problem. The PFNA method also requires the use of an on-site nuclear accelerator to produce the fast neutrons. A proposed configuration for an explosive detection device based on the PFNA concepts is shown in Figure 5.

FIGURE 5

PULSED-FAST NEUTRON ACTIVATION DEVICE FOR LUGGAGE SCREENING

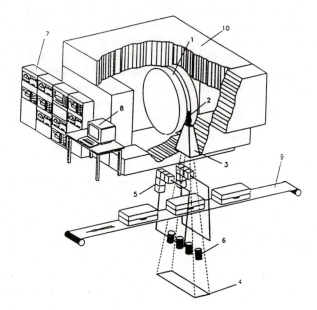

4. Photon Activation

This technique involves the use of a powerful electron linear accelerator that is used to produce x-rays with a high energy limit that is sufficient to produce unusual isotopes of elements such as nitrogen. After a momentary bombardment of a suitcase with an intense broad spectrum of x-rays, the suitcase is moved into a complex detector system that detects the radiation produced by the decay of an isotope such as nitrogen-13. The practical aspects in operating a powerful electron accelerator, the radiation associated with the accelerator, and the utter destruction of any film or other radiation sensitive materials in the luggage could very well make this method unacceptable for baggage inspection.

5. Nuclear Resonant Absorption

In this approach a beam of protons is used to bombard a carbon-13 target that produces gamma rays which at a specific angle with respect to the proton beam have precisely the right energy to be absorbed by nitrogen nuclei. This is again a technology which requires complex and expensive instrumentation that would be difficult to operate reliably in an airport environment. A conceptual layout for a nuclear resonant absorption system is shown in Figure 6.

Among all of the possible nuclear detection techniques TNA appears most likely to play a significant role.

X-Ray Methods

Advanced x-ray devices appear to provide at least six more attractive options for explosive detection.

1. Dual Energy X-Ray Devices

In a dual x-ray energy device, x-rays are produced at two different energies. The differences in absorption between the x-rays of the two different energies then allows the determination of the average atomic number of the object being scanned. This selectivity in atomic number for any particular object within a suitcase allows identification of several plastic explosives because their average atomic number values fall within a very narrow range with relatively little interference from other common materials.

The computer based analysis of this dual energy information is very complex. The data analysis program first identifies specific objects

FIGURE 6

NUCLEAR RESONANT ABSORPTION SYSTEM (CONCEPTUAL)

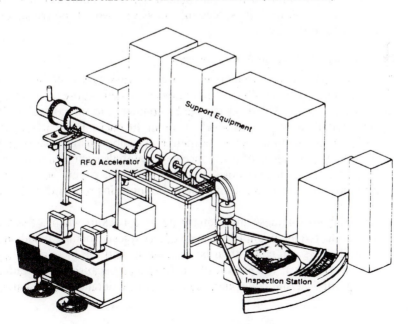

throughout the suitcase and then proceeds to analyse these objects one at a time. The stepwise analysis of each object provides a detailed atomic number determination of each pixel within the object and utilises this information to check for the signature of explosives. In normal operation the computation requires only one or two seconds and the final analysis is presented within a six-second time interval. The contrast enhancement capability of this new device with its extremely narrow re-solution and average atomic number determination make it a very powerful device for explosive detection. It can also be used to identify for example materials associated with detonators. It is clear that the use of modern computational techniques and analysis algorithms makes a significant improvement to explosive detection devices.

2. Backscatter X-Ray

X-rays that pass through an object are most effectively absorbed by mat-erials composed of atoms with high atomic number. Thus traditional screening systems are extremely effective for detecting metal objects such as hand guns. However, x-rays are not effectively absorbed by the low atomic number materials of which plastic explosives are typically composed. However, materials containing low atomic number elements can effectively scatter x-rays back towards their source. Thus backscat-ter x-rays can in principle be used for the detection of plastic explosives. However, the ability of this technique to discriminate explosives from other low atomic number materials such as paper has not been demon-strated. The method, if successful, however would be relatively inexpensive to deploy.

3. Extremely Low-Dose X-Ray Systems

Devices which use an extremely low dose of x-rays have been proposed for scanning personnel. One of these devices would expose a passenger to only 2 or 3 micro REM, which can be compared to the normal back-ground radiation at ground level of about 10 micro REM per hour. These devices are impressive for their remarkable imaging capability and reveal the presence of any concealed materials such as metals and plastics. Since all chequebooks, billfolds (wallets), paper, books, etc. would show up with such a scan it might be confusing to identify what is being seen.

The best use of these units might be as a backup when a vapour system indicated the possible presence of an explosive being carried on a person. This person could then be scanned to find the location of the suspicious object. If the person refused the scan because of the 'radia-tion exposure' he/she could then be subject to a detailed body search.

The deployment of such extremely low dose x-ray scanning systems will be critically dependent on public acceptance.

4. Coherent X-Ray Scattering

This x-ray method which has been tested only under ideal conditions, utilises x-ray diffraction. The technique differs from usual diffraction methods in the sense that the data is taken at a fixed angle and the energy spectrum recorded while in more conventional diffraction experiments the x-ray energy is fixed and the angle is changed. A conceptual arrangement of a coherent x-ray system is shown in Figure 7. The explosive materials are identified because of their molecular crystalline structure even though they may be present as powders, and mixed with plasticisers of various kinds. The powder diffraction patterns for different explosives have been analysed and compared to other materials, and discrimination of the explosive compounds is excellent. If the results obtained under laboratory conditions can be obtained in an airport environment, this method of structure identification of explosives could be a powerful and relatively inexpensive means of getting a

FIGURE 7

COHERENT X-RAY SYSTEM (CONCEPTUAL)

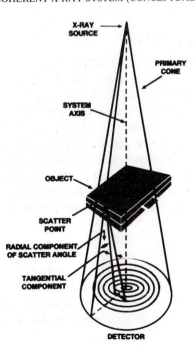

specific explosive signature. This approach appears to be extremely promising and has significant long-range potential.

5. Dual Energy X-Ray Computed Tomography

Dual Energy Computed Tomography (CT) has the potential to determine the shape, atomic number, and density of objects in luggage. It holds significant promise for a detailed analysis of suspect bags identified by other primary screening methods. Typically the object is imaged one cross section at a time and a three-dimensional image if required is made up of a series of these slices.

CT imaging is probably too expensive, and is not fast enough at present to be used as a primary screening tool but developments on the horizon show promise for increasing throughput.

6. Characteristic X-Ray

The characteristic x-ray method is based on the sharp increase in x-ray absorption at characteristic energies for each chemical element. Because these devices detect elements other than nitrogen, they could be combined with other detection devices to increase effectively the probability of detecting components of an explosive device such as detonators and batteries. This capability could be incorporated into existing x-ray systems.

Magnetic Resonance Methods

Nuclear Magnetic Resonance (NMR) imaging and relaxation time measurements may also play a specialised role in explosive detection. Although use of NMR to scan the heterogeneous mixture of materials that might turn up in luggage appears to be unlikely, specialised applications such as determining the nature of liquids in bottles without opening the bottles could be readily accomplished with NMR.

Nuclear quadruple resonance does not require the presence of a magnetic field, and can be used to detect resonant absorptions which are highly characteristic of specific explosive materials. Nuclear quadruple resonance using handheld surface coils has promise as a screening device for passengers.

Vapour Detectors

Different technical approaches have been used to build extraordinary sensitive vapour detection devices. These devices typically consist of a sampler for collecting and concentrating the available vapour, and methods for chemical analysis, discrimination, detection, and reporting the existence or the identify of an explosive. The collection devices include handheld probes for collecting vapour surrounding the article of interest as well as booths which are in various stages of development and testing. The vapour is frequently concentrated by condensation on surfaces of different composition. Detection may be based on ion mobility and electron capture, mass spectrometry, chromatography, or pyrolysis followed by optical detection of chemiluminescent reactions for chemical analysis and detection. Figure 8 illustrates a vapour detection booth used in conjunction with other screening methods at a terminal checkpoint.

Although these devices can detect an extremely low concentration of vapour, the amount of material available for detection from high explosives which are the largest threat still appears to be well below the sensitivity of these devices. However, since typical military and commercial explosives contain a variety of contaminants, binders, and impurities, vapours emitted from these components may be possible targets. Vapour detection devices appear to have the capability of detecting particulates found on objects that are contaminated in the course of handling explosives. This capability could add significant value in an overall explosive detection strategy.

FIGURE 8

VAPOUR DETECTION BOOTH AT TERMINAL CHECKPOINT

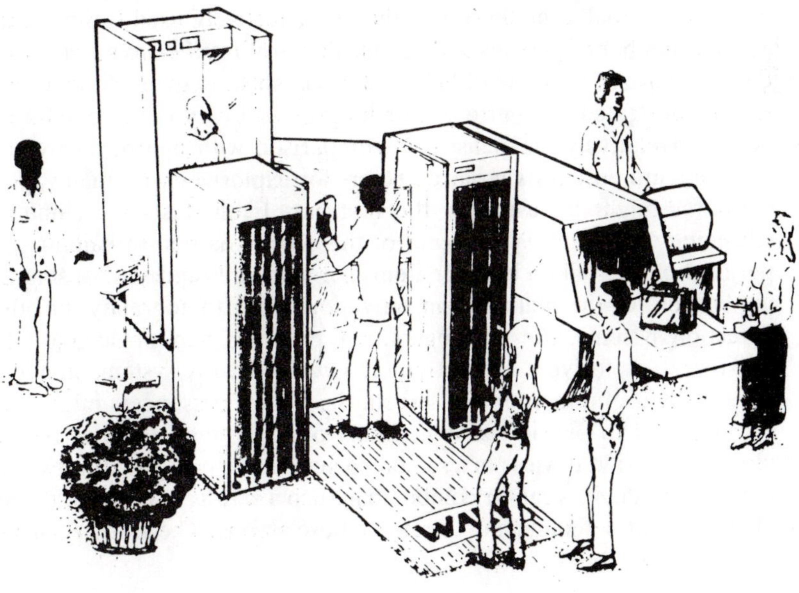

Each of the bulk and vapour methods discussed above has significant limitations and vulnerabilities to counter measures. However, the growing ensemble of different methods taken together represents a very significant capability. The emergence of this array of options is the result of a long term and consistent investment in research and development by the Federal Aviation Administration in the United States, corresponding agencies abroad, and individual vendors.

D. Systems Issues

1. Search Strategy

Given the large volume of luggage and passengers that must be dealt with and considering the extremely low probability of a true positive on any search and the associated high probability that any given bag or passenger will be passed on any screen, a succession of screening stages appears to be warranted. There does not appear to be any single detection technology that can provide a probability of detection, and a probability of false alarm that will have both a significant effect on reducing the threat and an acceptable impact on airport operations. An inexpensive and high-throughput initial screen (with high probability of detection) is required to eliminate most of the numerous passengers and objects that have low probability of posing a threat. More expensive and technically capable methods can then be effectively used to screen the smaller number of persons and objects that are classified as suspicious in the first cut. An example of how such a search strategy might be organised is illustrated in Figure 9. For luggage and cargo, advanced x-ray systems (relatively inexpensive in comparison with neutron activation systems) and perhaps vapour detectors for explosives with high vapour pressures might be used for the first cut. Even if such preliminary screening eliminated 90 per cent of the objects as non-threatening, 10 per cent of one billion baggage items per year still represents a staggering burden for thermal neutron activation, x-ray tomography, or other detection systems. For passengers, risk profiling, vapour detectors for low-threat explosives, and extremely low dose x-ray systems might be potentially useful in an initial screen. Suspicious passengers might then be subjected to physical search. Many other arrangements of the explosive detection devices in a screening system are possible. It is evident that various devices can be combined in such a way as to improve the net probability of detection and to resolve false alarms. The system can also be organised to optimise throughput and minimise cost for a given probability of detection. The trade-offs involved in optimising the systems architecture are sufficiently complex that a modelling and simulation capability for such systems would have significant value.

The implementation of any search strategy must recognise the dynamic nature of the technology and of the threat. For example, terrorists could switch to non-nitrogen containing explosives to thwart detection by devices based on sensing nitrogen in the explosive molecule. In this case, a well-configured system would have a high probability of being sensitive to some other aspect of the explosive device. The architecture of explosive detection devices should have sufficient flexibility to allow for new technologies to be introduced, and new threats to be countered.

2. Hardening vs. Detection

As long as the possibility exists that explosive material can be brought on board an aircraft by unsuspecting carriers or in stowed luggage the system is forced to deal with the explosive material itself. Since any

FIGURE 9

HYPOTHETICAL SYSTEMS ARCHITECTURE FOR EXPLOSIVE DETECTION

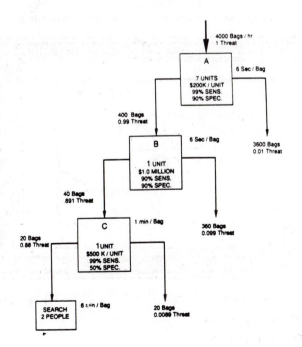

FIGURE 10

TYPICAL AIRCRAFT CARGO LOAD

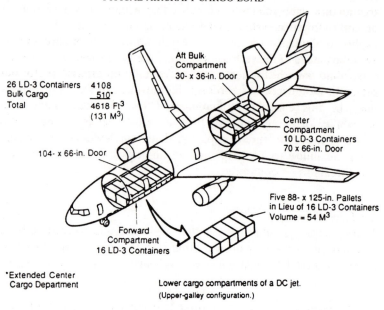

Lower cargo compartments of a DC jet.
(Upper-galley configuration.)

FIGURE 11

SCHEMATIC DESIGN OF HARDENED LUGGAGE CONTAINER (HLC)

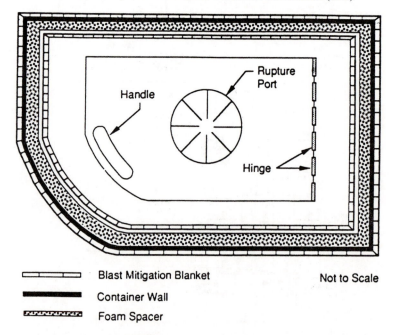

detection system can fail to detect the material there is some virtue in hardening the environment – certainly the luggage compartment – so that an explosion of any given amount of material is less likely to have disastrous consequences. Since hardening could increase the quantity of explosive required to destroy an aircraft, hardening can have an import-ant effect on the detectability of the explosive device.

Because of the substantial effect of weight on aircraft performance, only a limited degree of hardening is possible. However, it is possible that a degree of hardening that would have only a negligible effect on aircraft performance might nevertheless sufficiently increase the amount of material needed to destroy the aircraft so that the detection task would be considerably simplified. If some degree of hardening could raise the necessary amount of explosive from a barely detectable level to a readily detectable one, then hardening might be well worth while.

It may be possible that relatively straightforward and inexpensive modifications of aircraft baggage containers could substantially improve their capability to withstand the pressures produced by the detonation of small explosive charges. Modifications such as reinforcing the walls and seams using composite materials and perhaps adding lightweight compressible padding could substantially harden baggage containers to the effects of small explosive charges. Although not all aircraft are

FIGURE 12

TIME-PRESSURE PROFILES FOR HARDENED LUGGAGE CONTAINERS

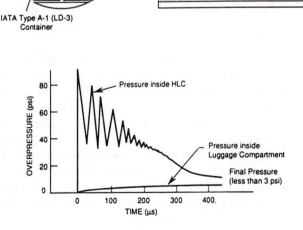

Approximate pressure calculations for a DC-10 configuration.

loaded with luggage containers, the larger aircraft in international service are typically loaded as shown in Figure 10. One approach to hardening such containers as shown in Figure 11, while the modification to the time-pressure profile in hardened test configurations is shown in Figure 12. It now appears possible that such approaches to luggage container hardening could play a significant role in the future of commercial aircraft security.

3. Low Technology Improvements

Some relatively low technology improvements that could add considerable value to the aircraft security system appear possible in current passenger and luggage management systems. For example, positive bag-to-passenger matching could have a significant impact on reducing the threat. This could be done using a variety of bar code or magnetic strip encoding schemes that would allow a rapid and positive reconciliation of passenger boarding and bag loading. Curb side check-in areas could also be equipped with simple encoding technology. This approach would greatly improve security for probably acceptable cost and aggravation. Maintaining control of the luggage of passengers who might leave the aircraft after luggage is loaded or at intermediate stops should be possible.

Clever use of existing systems can also add considerable value. For example, there is no reason why in times of higher tension, passengers cannot be asked to segregate items in their luggage, for example, placing electronic items, or items containing batteries in separate containers for separate screening. Local initiatives and changes in configuration make the screening system less predictable, and therefore add to the potential deterrence.

4. Explosive and Detonator Tagging

Small quantities of materials added to explosives and detonators could make them observable by relatively inexpensive means. Several approaches would be straightforward to implement such as the use of radioactive markers and high-vapour pressure additives. Explosive manufacturers in most countries, including all major powers with a significant stake in commercial air transportation should be willing to comply with a tagging requirement if the costs are minimal and the additive has no detrimental effect on the explosive formula. Although there are many explosives and detonators already available to potential terrorists, beginning a tagging programme could substantially reduce the long-term future threat. Agreement on international regulations and standards for explosive and detonator tagging would make a long-term contribution to commercial aircraft security.

E. Strategic Elements of an Aircraft Security Program

There are several broad strategic elements that should be the basis for future commercial aircraft security programmes. It is clear, for example, that a comprehensive approach is required. The technical approaches to explosive detection must be integrated with programme in aircraft and luggage container hardening. The aircraft security system must be closely coupled with available intelligence and the screening system must be responsive to changes in threat. Human factors will play a crucial role in the effectiveness of the screening system and must be reflected as a major factor in the strategic planning, and any security system must be viable within the context of airport and air carrier operations at a sustainable cost.

There is a range of threats to commercial aircraft from large, relatively crude, readily detectable devices to highly sophisticated cleverly-concealed devices. It is important to consider that although some techniques might not be effective against the most sophisticated devices, they will provide a significant capability against less sophisticated devices and thereby add value to the security system and contribute to deterrence. It is also important to understand that the technology for explosive detection is rapidly evolving and this understanding must be incorporated into the strategic approach. It is useful to experiment in the field with systems that are perhaps not capable against the most sophisticated threats to understand human factors, and operating and maintenance issues so that the value from practical operating experience can be available for subsequent device design and improvement.

The most effective approach for explosive detection will typically involve different techniques organised in such a way as to optimise the probability of detection while minimising the impact on operations, and capital and operating cost. It is clear that trade-offs must be made between these desirable objectives, and that the problem is sufficiently complicated that the most desirable solution may not be self-evident. Modelling and simulation of the passenger and baggage screening processes for various detector system layouts will be of significant value. Such models should be available to air carriers, airport operators regulators, and airport designers.

Regulatory agencies such as the FAA should be responsible for creating regulations which specify the overall probability of detection for an airport screening system. Such regulations should require a probability of detection for given quantities of specific explosive types. Since no screening system can be expected to operate at a high probability of detection without penalties in cost and operational impact, the regulations must provide clear guidance for system engineering. The explicit choice of a probability of detection for design purposes is clearly an extraordinary sensitive matter. The regulatory body should also be responsible for certifying that equipment provided by manufacturers performs according to their advertised specifications. Finally, the regulatory body should be responsible for verifying (with enforcement authority) that systems in the field are indeed performing according to the regulatory requirements. However, neither the Congress nor the FAA, for example, in the United States should be involved in setting requirements for specific technical solutions. The individual air carriers and airport operators should have responsibility for organising the search strategy in such a way as to meet an overall probability of detection requirement, and they should have the flexibility to make the inevitable trade-offs between devices of different types supplied by different manufacturers to minimise cost and operational disruption. Rather than having specific technical solutions mandated, manufacturers should have the incentive to make continuing incremental improvements in technology and procedures.

ACKNOWLEDGEMENTS

Much of the material in this report is the result of the deliberations by the Committee on Commercial Aircraft Security of the National Research Council of the National Academy of Sciences of the USA. The author was Chairman of this Committee, whose membership included: Jonathan W. Amy (Purdue University), Alfred Blumstein (Carnegie-Mellon University), Arthur Fries (Institute for Defense Analyses), Stanley S. Hanna (Stanford University), Wilfred A. Jackson (University of North Dakota), Richard H. Judy (Richard H. Judy & Associates), Bruce Kowalski (University of Washington), David Milligan (Abbott Laboratories), Harold McNair (Virginia Polytechnic Institute), John R. Orr (Delta Airlines), John C. Sheehan (Massachusetts Institute of Technology), Howard E. Simmons, Jr. (E.I. duPont de Nemours & Co.), Norman Slagg (Picatinny Arsenal), Harvey E. Wegner (Brookhaven National Labs), with the assistance of Stanley M. Barkin, Robert E. Schafrik, and Janice M. Prisco of the National Materials Advisory Board staff and Jennelle Derrickson and William Wall, liaison representatives from the FAA Technical Center in Atlantic City, New Jersey.

Designing an Effective International Aviation Security System

PAUL WILKINSON

International reform of aviation security is vital in the light of continuing vulnerability to sabotage bombing and other threats. Radical innovation and broad vision are needed to design an effective system, but it is feasible. (Many predicted that the US anti-hijack measures introduced in 1972 would be unworkable: in fact they were highly successful.) The author argues for enhanced security coordination at national and international levels, especially in the fields of counter-terrorism intelligence, radically enhanced explosive detection systems, airport security procedures, and security staff quality, and a major programme to help poorer countries to upgrade their airport security.

Terrorists make it their business to threaten the most basic of human rights – the right to life. The civil aviation industry has since its inception been dedicated to protecting the safety of passengers and crews. Indeed it is the incredibly good safety record of the world's airlines that has helped to make air travel such a phenomenally successful mode of transport and one of the fastest growing industries in the world. Therefore, even if there were no legal obligations on airlines and airports to provide security, most of those working in the industry would accept that there is an inescapable moral obligation resting on both governments and the civil aviation community to collaborate in taking all possible measures to protect passengers, crews, ground staff, and the public in general, against the scourge of aviation terrorism.

In addition to this overwhelming argument from moral principle there is now a compelling case to be made for an effective security system on grounds of the commercial interests of the civil aviation industry. The 1991 Gulf War has demonstrated that if the public develop a real fear of flying and no longer trust the will and capability of governments and aviation authorities to deter and prevent terrorist attacks, they will desert the airways in droves. In the first week of the war the Association of European Airlines claimed that its members had lost 25 per cent of their traffic. *Airline Business* estimated that the industry as a whole was losing approximately $1.5 billion per month in the immediate aftermath of the war. There is no doubt that the industry has been hard hit by the recession, and this also helped the slow recovery after the Gulf War. Nevertheless, the industry has every reason to fear the effects of any future major conflict in the Middle East and the concomitant threat of increased terrorism. What counts is the public's perception of the risks involved. Whereas airlines used to argue that they could not afford effective security, they must now realise that they cannot afford not to have an effective aviation security system.

Liberal democratic governments and public have other powerful reasons, in addition to the principle of protecting the lives of the innocent, which should spur them to help create effective aviation security. All democratic societies have a vital interest in the maintenance of lawful authority and the rule of law. By resorting to the bomb and the bullet terrorists brutally defy the authority of the law. It would be absurd to argue that individual acts of aviation terrorism threaten the survival of the state. Yet it would also be foolish to deny that any democratic state has a vital interest in the defeat and eradication of groups that commit major crimes such as terrorism, and that weakness in responding to terrorist attacks may lead to the dangerous policy of making major concessions to terrorists and may encourage other terrorist groups to use similar tactics. As part of democratic society the civil aviation industry shares a common interest in the suppression of terrorism.

There is another major argument for establishing an effective aviation security system, and it is one which should add far greater urgency to our efforts. This is the key point that the threat posed by aviation terrorists has become infinitely more lethal over the past decade. Twenty years ago the major terrorist threat to aviation was hijacking. This problem has by no means disappeared: the 1988 Kuwait Airlines hijacking demonstrated extreme cunning and ruthlessness on the part of the terrorists, who proved more than a match for the aviation authorities in the countries where they landed. However, the danger of hijacking has been shapely reduced by a combination of simple but effective technology and procedures; improved international cooperation, including such measures as the US Cuba Hijack Pact which closed down Cuba as a terrorist bolt-hole; and the deterrent effect of dramatically successful commando-style rescues of airline passengers and crews at Entebbe, Mogadishu, and elsewhere, in which the hijackers were killed.

Over the past decade terrorists have switched the emphasis away from hijacking to the far more cowardly tactic of smuggling a bomb on board an airliner and timing it to explode in mid air. As was demonstrated in the horror of the Pan Am explosion over Lockerbie in 1988 and the UTA explosion over Niger the following year, when a bomb explodes on an airliner at an altitude of over 30,000 feet, the passengers and crew have no chance of survival. It is mass murder in the skies. Modern plastic explosives and sophisticated timing mechanisms provide an ideal weapon for terrorists for this purpose. The huge payloads of modern jumbo jets serve to maximise the carnage. In the decade 1960–69 there were 9 sabotage attacks against civil aircraft, resulting in 286 deaths. In 1980–89 there were 12 attacks causing a total of 1144 deaths, a tripling of the number of fatalities per incident over the 20 years period. By the end of the 1980s aviation terrorism rivalled technical failure and pilot error as a cause of fatalities in civil aviation. Nor should we overlook the potential for very much higher levels of casualties if an airliner were to be blown up above a major centre of population.

As I argued in my 1989 report, *The Lessons of Lockerbie*, the sad fact is that our aviation security systems had become hopelessly outdated by the 1980s. They were geared solely to dealing with the hijacking threat. The magnetometer archways and x-ray machines introduced in the early 1970s were designed to prevent passengers from smuggling metallic objects, potential hijack weapons, on board aircraft. Although the sabotage bomb threat was clearly evident by the mid-1980s, most of the world's aviation authorities had made little of no effort to put in place the explosive detection systems, stringent baggage reconciliation procedures, effective perimeter and access controls, and other measures necessary to counter it.

The only airline that proved fully capable of coping with this new challenge was El Al. They compensated for the lack of an effective explosive detection system (EDS) by exploiting their unique assets in counter-terrorism intelligence, their well-honed techniques of passenger profiling and interrogation and their comprehensive manual searches of luggage. You will recall that is was an alert El Al security officer at Heathrow who discovered the bomb Nizar Hindawi had duped his pregnant Irish girlfriend into taking aboard an El Al jet in 1986. Yet although all airlines have much to learn from El Al in terms of intelligence, motivation and the importance of the human factor in aviation security, it would be totally impracticable for the major aviation states to adopt El Al's overall approach. The Israeli airline has a much smaller total air traffic, and no short haul flights, and its passengers are sufficiently motivated to accept much earlier check-in times than would be customary for American or European airlines.

Designing an Effective Aviation Security System

In designing an effective aviation security system, I suggest that we should be encouraged and inspired by the lessons of America's response to the hijacking plague of the late 1960s and early 1970s. If you examine the statistics of worldwide hijacking in 1968 to 1972 you will find that in 1969, 1971, and 1972 almost half the hijack attempts originated in the USA. In the peak year, 1969, no less than 37 of the 82 hijacking attempts worldwide took place aboard flights originating in the USA. The programme of anti-hijack measures adopted by the American authorities in 1972 was audacious and was inspired by the broad vision of the man who was appointed Director of Aviation Security, Lieutenant General Benjamin Davis.

Lieutenant General Davis immediately recognised that measures taken to combat the hijacker in the air were merely palliative: once the hijacker was airborne it was too late. He therefore adopted the policy of thorough screening and searches at the boarding gate to prevent the hijacker and his weapons getting aboard. Davis and his advisers were told that this radical scheme would not work, that the airlines and the airports would refuse to cooperate, and that the American public would not accept universal boarding gate security checks. The critics were proved wrong on all counts. The secret of making the checks acceptable to the travelling public was to ensure that adequate staff and machines were available to check passengers very rapidly, thus ensuring that any delays that did occur happened at the check-in desks or through unavoidable technical, weather, or air traffic control holdups and not at security. The airports and airlines cooperated to make the new system work, initially because they had no other choice. The 1973 legislation made the boarding gate security measures mandatory throughout America. However the aviation industry was fairly rapidly won over to the value of the new system. In 1973, the year after its introduction, US hijack attempts dropped from 29 to 3, and in the course of boarding gate searches 3,500lb of high explosives, 2000 guns and 23,000 knives and other lethal weapons were found.

It is hardly necessary to remind you that the American airport security measures were so successful that other major aviation countries rapidly adopted similar measures, and eventually they spread worldwide. We can therefore learn some useful lessons from the US anti-hijacking measures which could be applied to the design of an effective system to combat the sabotage bombing threat: (i) the system was centrally designed and co-ordinated and was made mandatory for all airlines and airports throughout the USA; (ii) the system used effective widely available and affordable technology for boarding gate screening of all passengers and carry-on luggage; (iii) the system was designed to be fully compatible with a rapid throughput of passengers without any significant loss of passenger comfort or convenience, and hence with no reduction in the commercial viability of the industry.

Lessons from Experience

Let us bear these lessons in mind in defining the essential components of an aviation security system capable of dealing with today's infinitely more complex and dangerous problems of international aviation security. It would be foolish to underestimate the difficulties involved in getting our present governments and the aviation industry to act effectively at both national and international levels. Bismarck once said 'Fools say they learn from experience. I prefer to learn from others' experience.' Let us hope that other countries do not have to experience more tragic outrages on the scale of Lockerbie before they are mobilised to take the necessary action.

The most important general lesson we must all learn from the recent history of aviation terrorism is never again to allow the terrorists to get so far ahead of the world's airport security system. We should already be anticipating the tactics that the terrorists are likely to use once the method of sabotage bombing has been blocked. For example, we should already be devising ways of preventing terrorists from obtaining and using surface-to-air missiles against civil aviation. And we should be planning defensive and counter-measures to deal with the possible terrorist use of chemical and biological weapons against such targets as airport terminals.

Essential Components of an Effective Aviation Security System

The first requirement is the establishment of strong national aviation security systems, particularly in the major civil aviation countries, the G7 states and Russia. Effective national systems are the essential building-blocks of any worthwhile international cooperation. Each national security system should under the control of a powerful lead agency with the tasks of assisting government in the formulation of aviation security policy, and the overall-direction and co-ordination of all the organisations in both public and private sectors which have a role in implementing the aviation security programme. The lead agency should be backed by strong regulatory powers and the necessary resources, including trained manpower, necessary to monitor, inspect and regulate all aspects of aviation security. It should in addition have the task of evaluating the overall effectiveness of the security policy and recommending any necessary changes to government.

There is much evidence to suggest that the commercial deregulation of airlines has had beneficial consequences for the air traveller. Opening up a far greater choice of services and making vigorous competition for routes and passengers has compelled airlines and airports to strive for a larger market share by offering better quality services at more attractive prices. Experience shows, however, that it would be foolish and irresponsible to leave matters such as air safety and security to the vagaries of the market. As the Americans have shown, a strong regulatory agency is absolutely vital it standards of security are to be properly enforced and leadership in research and development and policy direction is to be provided. Many countries do not have a sufficiently powerful lead agency for aviation security. Many suffer from a confusion of overlapping agencies, often working at cross purposes.

Yet if aviation security is going to be really effective reforms and enhancement at purely national level are not going to be enough. It is no good making Britain and the USA into fortresses of enhanced airport security while other countries airports remain wide open to the sabotage bomber and even in many cases, the moderately resourceful would-be hijacker. Terrorist organisations will seek out the weakest links, for example using interline baggage from an African airport with negligible security to get a bomb on board an aircraft belonging to the flag airline of their chosen target state.

Sadly, we are still a very long way from achieving a global civil aviation security organisation with real powers of enforcement. The International Civil Aviation Organisation (ICAO) has just completed a very useful revision of its Annexe 17 security standards, and a useful multilateral convention on the tagging of explosive substances has just been negotiated under its aegis. However, the world civil aviation body cannot proceed any faster than the broad consensus of its member states permits. And it must be admitted that most states show no enthusiasm for giving ICAO much greater direct authority and control over aviation security. It should also be remembered that the G7 states themselves share great scepticism about a greatly enhanced ICAO security role, because they are aware that the organisation contains states which are active state sponsors and supporters of terrorism. Hence, in the medium term the best mechanism for enhanced international coordination in aviation security appears to be the G7 group of states, the major industrialised countries which also happen to be the world's key aviation states, with the possible addition of Russia.

The 1991 Gulf War experience dramatically demonstrated the value of this informal grouping of states in the counter-terrorism field. The main reason that Saddam's plans to use international terrorism as an auxiliary weapon in the Gulf War failed so dismally is that they were pre-empted or thwarted so effectively through the combined efforts of the coalition governments and their counter-terrorism agencies. It is true that there were almost 200 incidents linked to the Gulf War recorded in the six weeks of hostilities. Yet the majority of these were low-level, even amateurish, in character, and caused very few casualties. There were no serious attacks on major civil aviation targets. The considerably enhanced security measures adopted by airports, airlines and other potential targets clearly paid off. It is also clear that the expulsion of key Iraqi personnel based in Western countries, under diplomatic and other cover, removed many of those who would have had a leading role in co-ordinating and initiating terrorist activity against coalition targets. No doubt some mistakes were made by the Western intelligence services. But their overall contribution was an excellent illustration of the value of high calibre intelligence and surveillance in countering terrorism. Their success provides a useful model for closer intelligence and counter-terrorism against the longer-term threat of aviation terrorism in 'peacetime'. Skilled work by the intelligence services and police of the major aviation countries working in concert can tackle the terrorist threat before it actually reaches the boarding gates or the airport perimeter areas.

Yet with the best will in the world and the most sophisticated use of intelligence resources some terrorists will succeed in reaching the airports. At this point all will depend on the capabilities and efficiency of the airport security system. The system must be able to deal effectively with the continuing threat of aircraft hijacking, the potentially more lethal threat of sabotage bombing and numerous other forms of aviation terrorism such as bombing and shooting attacks on airport terminals and armed attacks against aircraft on the ground. It is a serious error to concentrate attention solely on the boarding gate and terminal security problems. Perimeter security, and access control to airside, cargo storage and ground servicing areas, must all be included as they are crucial aspects of the overall security system. While it is encouraging to record that perimeter security and access control have received much closer attention in Britain, the USA and some other countries recently, the bad news is that there are scores of airports, especially in the poorest countries, where perimeter security and access control to vulnerable areas simply does not exist.

The threat of sabotage bombing can only be effectively countered by a comprehensive multipronged approach. The security system must be capable of preventing bombs being smuggled in through checked baggage, carry-on luggage, via the person of the passenger, through air cargo, and through airport services of all kinds.

Even our most modern airports are sadly lacking in an effective explosives detection system (EDS) to counter the sabotage threat. It is clear that there is no single technology which can provide a panacea. Much more R & D is still needed to get the best machines. Thermal Neutron Analysis (TNA) is available in prototype, but there are still great doubts about its ability to reliably detect qualities of plastic explosive of the amount believed to have been used to blow up Pan Am 103 while keeping the false alarm rate down to manageable levels. TNA machines are also extremely costly and are too large and heavy to be sited easily in existing airport security areas. More research is needed to refine this technology, and further work is also required to perfect fast neutron technology which is a promising possible alternative. Enhanced x-ray is an extremely valuable and far cheaper technology, already commercially available using a number of different techniques, including back-scatter and CT.

The difficulty with over-reliance on these machines is that it is often very difficult to interpret the image accurately. Considerable operator training skills, and aptitude may be needed to get full value from these technologies. There are also interesting new developments in explosive detection by 'sniffing' explosive vapour or residues. The available techniques range from mass spectometry to chemiluminescence. Unfortunately none of these methods is wholly reliable, especially if the terrorist is clever enough to find a means of sealing the explosives, because all these techniques depend on the availability of explosive vapour or residues. It has been shown that a sniffer dog does far better than a machine, but dogs get tired and can be distracted, and in any case it is not really practicable to use them for all routine pre-boarding gate security checks!

To sum up on the existing state of EDS: the aviation authorities should be designing a standard security 'tunnel' for use in all airports with a combination of different types of technology rather than over-dependence on one machine. Because of the investment needed for the large-scale production of security equipment, and the huge advantages of exploiting the best available technologies in the world market, the G7 states' aviation authorities should be planning a concerted approach to commissioning the best available EDS machines for the task, throughout their airport systems. Today the best package would probably include: (a) reliable and affordable enhanced x-rays; (b) reliable and affordable vapour sniffers; and (c) *either* (subject to satisfactory testing and improvement of prototypes) fast neutron activation *or* resonance absorption of gamma rays, depending on which technology proves the most reliable and affordable.

However good the technology deployed for airport security may be, and it must be of the highest efficiency, the security system will fail unless we ensure that we design into our system the best possible security procedures, combining effectiveness with maximum speed, comfort and convenience for the air traveller. These procedures must be approved and monitored and enforced in detail. Sanctions by the security regulatory agencies must be enforced in all cases where these procedures are violated. The procedures must cover:

- efficient passenger identification and screening, ensuring that all 'high selected' passengers are checked out comprehensively before boarding;
- efficient screening of *all* carry-on and hold luggage;
- stringent procedures for reconciliation of every item of baggage carried with a passenger boarded on the same flight: there should be no excuse for failure to operate a truly effective baggage reconciliation system as a foolproof computerized system has now been designed, using the International Air Transport Association bar code system and a laser reader at the point of loading, to ensure that no unauthorized unaccompanied bag is loaded on to an aircraft (N.B., this system is extremely cost effective as it will save the industry millions of dollars in misrouted baggage)
- efficient screening of all air freight, including diplomatic baggage;
- strict separation of all transit passengers from non-transit passengers and 'meeters and greeters';
- stringent airside security, including proper protection of aircraft on the ground, access control, perimeter protection;
- efficient screening of all electrical equipment carried on board aircraft, and refusal to carry items of equipment which cannot be properly checked.

Most of these procedural requirements are covered in ICAO's own manual of recommended procedures. Sadly these have only the status of recommendations, however. Security-conscious governments should concert pressure on ICAO to introduce a proper international aviation security inspectorate with powers to carry out spot checks on all international airports, and to report back to the ICAO's security committee.

Any country that persistently fails to brings it security up to ICAO minimum standards should then be made subject to official aviation sanctions by the international aviation community. The US government has already demonstrated the potential of this kind of pressure when President Reagan issued his 'Advisory' warning to US passengers to avoid Athens airport. As a result the Greek authorities made strenuous efforts to try to beef up airport security: they realised they had much to lose by the sudden decline in American visitors.

However, none of the measures we have so far discussed will have any real security value unless we also radically enhance the human factor in security. This is where we can learn invaluable lessons from the El Al security system. Their top security people are fully trained intelligence officers with the professional background knowledge of political terrorism, international politics, and aviation security, to provide expert management and operational supervision. All their security personnel are well trained, motivated and disciplined. They are regarded, quite rightly, as important – indeed indispensable-members of the Israel civil aviation industry and not, as so often happens in America and European Community countries, as a Cinderella service, poorly paid, poorly trained, and poorly motivated.

There is not space in this brief study to describe the design of these essential components of aviation security in detail. But it will already be clear to you that in my view the aviation security systems of even the major aviation states have a long way to go before they measure up to the challenge of modern terrorism. At least countries such as Britain, the USA, and Germany, are moving in the right direction. We are beginning to put some of key components in place. A far more desperate need exists among the poorer nations of the Third World. Even if they recognise the woeful vulnerability of their airports (and many do) they simply do not possess the necessary funds and technical expertise to get their national aviation systems up to scratch. To overcome this problem I propose that the G7 states combine forces with the aerospace and airline industry, with help of a modest passenger security levy to set up an international aviation security fund which would provide soft loans, grants-in-aid and subsidised airport security equipment to those countries which quite genuinely cannot afford it. In addition I urge the launching of a major international programme to train the airport staff of low income countries in all the techniques and skills of aviation security, so that they can provide a core of key security staff throughout the world's airports. The International Aviation Management Training Institute of Montreal has been doing a superb job in attempting this task, so far as its modest resources will allow. Some G7 states – the

USA, Canada, Britain and France – also do a great deal through bilateral training and technical assistance. But this is a drop in the ocean compared to what is needed. I urge a major international programme in aviation security education to ensure that new technologies and stringent procedures to protect lives are spread rapidly throughout the world, and are not confined to the airports and airlines of the rich countries. The investment would be doubly worthwhile: it would sharply reduce the threat of aviation terrorism against innocent life and it would increase the trust and confidence of the travelling public, thus encouraging the continued healthy growth of the world civil aviation industry.

Do our Governments and the Aviation Industry have the Will to Act?

The proposals for establishing an effective aviation security system, very briefly outlined here, are radical and ambitious, but they are urgently needed. Moreover, provided that governments and the aviation industry have the will to act, these proposals are entirely feasible. We have noted how the huge aviation system of the USA developed a radical and astonishingly effective approach to combating the hijacking plague, when many critics advised that this would be impossible. We have observed how the coalition allies during the Gulf War achieved an astonishing degree of success in co-ordinating their counter-terrorism efforts against Saddam Hussein.

What are the prospects of radically enhancing global aviation security in the longer term? The true litmus test will be the Western states' consistency and courage in maintaining a firm and effective policy against international terrorism in all its forms. The general principles of the firm hardline strategy, which I have long advocated for the liberal state, and which have the best track record in reducing terrorism, are:

- no surrender to the terrorists, and an absolute determination to defeat terrorism within the framework of the rule of law and the democratic process;
- no deals and no concessions, even in the face of the most severe intimidation and blackmail;
- an intensified effort to bring terrorists to justice by prosecution and conviction before courts of law;
- tough measures to penalise the state sponsors who give terrorist movements safe haven, explosives, cash and moral and diplomatic support.

- a determination never to allow terrorist intimidation to block or derail international diplomatic efforts to resolve major political conflicts in strife-torn regions, such as the Middle East: in many such areas terrorism has become a major threat to peace and stability, and its suppression therefore is in the common interests of international society.

The battle to protect civil aviation passengers and crews can only be won if the liberal democracies have the will and courage to win the broader struggle against the scourge of international terrorism. Our freedom of the airways is ultimately dependent on our ability to preserve the freedom of society as a whole. Dedicating ourselves to the vigorous pursuits of these goals would be the best memorial to the passengers and crew of Pan Am 103 and the thousands of other innocent victims of international terrorist crime. Let us mobilise the industry and the public to help give governments the will to act.

Aviation Security: A Legislator's Perspective

DAVID MARSHALL MP

David Marshall, Labour MP for Glasgow Shettleston since 1979, was Chairman of the House of Commons Select Committee on Transport from 1987 until 1992 and has twice been involved in inquiries into airport security. Here he gives examples of the work of a Parliamentary Select Committee, its powers – or lack of them – and what good can come out of Select Committee Inquiries. British Select Committees may not be nearly as powerful as Congressional Committees in the USA but they can be influential and do play a vital role in highlighting matters of public interest. As David Marshall points out nothing concentrates the mind of a senior civil servant or government minister more than the prospect of being grilled for several hours by a Select Committee, whether or not it is in front of the TV cameras and in full view of the nation.

Another Lockerbie tragedy could happen at any time, anywhere in the world, even in Britain or the USA. What is surprising is not that it happened, but that there have not been many, many more than the other two or three such atrocities committed by terrorists. This, I suspect, is not due as much to excellent security as it is to lack of effort on the part of the terrorists. I have no evidence to support this statement and it is almost impossible to get any details of successful security operations which have been carried out.

Of course you will be told about the hundreds of potentially dangerous items confiscated temporarily, or even permanently, from passengers, but I have never yet heard of any frustrated bomb attempt in Britain, apart from the 1986 El Al case of the terrorist's girlfriend who was to be sacrificed. That incident received massive publicity and I have no reason to doubt that any other successes would have become public knowledge also.

It gives me no great pleasure to have said what I just said. I just do not believe that you can ever guarantee 100 per cent security, especially in the field of civil aviation. I do not seek to blame any one individual. It is more the nature of the industry and the tremendous difficulties facing security personnel.

However, I do believe that more could be done by governments, and it is small comfort to believe that the United Kingdom is one of the most security conscious countries with one of the better standards of security. It makes one shudder to think about the levels of security competence at some airports around the world.

The presence of armed guards or troops may be useful in the event of an armed assault on an airport but that has much less appeal to a highly sophisticated terrorist organisation than the opportunity to blow an airliner out of the sky and themselves onto the headlines of the world's media.

It is not my intention to make party political comments, the subject is far too serious to make cheap political capital. That was one of the good things about the last select committee – we very often crossed party political lines. In fact on many occasions the government members on the committee were much more severe on their ministers than we were.

I warmly welcome a seminar such as this, and hope that it could become an established conference or seminar held annually or biennially, to monitor the security situation, review progress – or the lack of it – and to make suggestions for improvements in the light of fresh information, or new technology. There is no reason why you could not have Cabinet ministers, civil servants, or aviation industry bosses along as guest speakers with question, answers, and discussion sessions.

I accepted the invitation to address this seminar with some trepidation. You are all academic experts of one kind or another with a far greater knowledge of the subject than I possess. When I arrived tonight my worst fears were confirmed. I am only a layman with a little experience. However, perhaps that very fact will bring you a different perspective on the subject, not an academic one more a man-in-the-street one, as well as giving you an insight into the parliamentary select committee system which I will explain in some detail.

Departmental select committees are set up to scrutinise the executive and its expenditure. They monitor the work of the respective department of state. In the case of transport that means anything to do with road, rail, air and sea and involves a very wide range of activities, some of which the committee have never yet had time to visit or look into. Select committees are set up by the House of Commons, and are answerable to the House, not to the government. They have powers to summon people before them and to call for relevant papers to be brought before them.

They normally consist of 11 members, reflecting the state of the parties in the House. All have a government majority. In the 1983 parliament, transport had 7 Tory, 3 Labour and 1 Liberal member, in 1987 it was 7 Tory and 4 Labour. Now it is 6 Tory and 5 Labour. Members are appointed for a parliament, that is, four or five years but can come off for various reasons. These are back-bench positions so on becoming a minister or shadow spokesman a member comes off a select committee. Some committees have opposition members as chairmen, and transport was one of these until July 1992, when it reverted to having a government member as chair, a decision which really upset me. My committee had worked well – it cut across party lines. To succeed, select committees must be consensual not confrontational and I believe we achieved that aim.

Staffing of select committees is inadequate. We have a full-time clerk, an administrative person, a secretary/typist, and a specialist assistant who is appointed on a two-year contract, renewable for a further two years, then has to resign and be replaced by someone else. We can and do appoint specialist advisers, usually academics, for the course of specific inquiries. These advisers are paid for the days worked on committee business. The committee elects its own chairman, draws up its own programme of inquiries, and when appropriate produces reports and makes recommendations. These reports are to the House of Commons and a response is then made via the Secretary of State. This can take days, weeks, or several months depending on the complexity of the report. We do not have any powers of implementation.

The greatest benefit of select committees is not in the number of recommendations which they have accepted by government, but in conducting inquiries, especially topical ones. This brings the subject matter into the public domain, more than ever now that many sessions are televised, and nothing concentrates the minds of civil servants and ministers more than having to appear before a select committee for two or three hours and explain what they are or are not doing.

A classic example of this was our inquiry into air traffic control safety and runway capacity a couple of years ago. The situation was a shambles when we announced our inquiry which lasted well over a year during which time the government and the civil aviation authority kept announcing more resources, new measures, new equipment, more staff in order to pre-empt many of the valid criticisms which they knew the committee could otherwise make. The end result was a considerable shake up and speed up which benefited everyone.

Another very worthwhile inquiry was into aircraft cabin safety in the light of the 1985 Manchester Airtours disaster. Other aviation inquiries have been into computer reservation systems and European air liberalisation.

In addition to general inquiries we have an annual inquiry into the public expenditure White Paper plans for transport during which the Permanent Secretary at the Department of Transport (DoT) is grilled by the Committee. We have annual sessions with the Chairman of British Rail, the Chief Executive of London Regional Transport and so on. We also have one-off sessions such as on cycling or Midland mainline electrification, or even being harangued by no less a person than Sam Skinner, then American Secretary for Transportation, when he visited the House of Commons in 1991 regarding liberalisation.

The Committee also makes visits to various places such as the Coast Guard operation at Falmouth, airline catering at Heathrow Airport, postbus services in the Isle of Skye, new signalling equipment at Inverness, air traffic control centres at Prestwick and West Drayton, the Channel Tunnel site at Folkestone and the new international terminal at Waterloo Railway Station, the new M40 Motorway in Oxfordshire during its construction, and so on.

One very interesting and beneficial aspect of select committee work is overseas visits. We went to the USA on two or three occasions and participated in university seminars at Harvard, Massachusetts Institute of Technology, and Berkeley. Americans are so much better at organising such think tanks which are excellent forums for debate. We should copy their example more often.

All of this takes time. Normally the committee meets on a Wednesday afternoon for about three hours. However, sometimes we have been involved in three inquiries simultaneously, and therefore can spend up to three days a week on select committee business. This is of course in addition to all our other duties as Members of Parliament and looking after our constituents and constituencies. Perhaps that is why the quorum for a committee is three and sometimes even that is difficult to achieve.

There is therefore a limit to what select committees can do and achieve. Nonetheless members can build up some expertise and select committee work can be amongst the most worthwhile activities in parliament. Change for the better can be achieved following select committee inquiries. No doubt new pension scheme legislation will flow from the Social Security Committee's inquiry into such schemes in light of the Maxwell scandal.

Returning to the reason for the present seminar can I stress that the value of academic effort into aviation security and terrorism cannot be overestimated. It is disappointing to note that there is a tendency to load organisations with representatives of all the vested interests, presumably on the basis that they consider themselves to be the only ones who know anything about the matter in question. A typical example was the working party on the policing of airports set up by the government which finished its work in October 1988 just before Lockerbie.

The composition was as follows:
Home Office Police Department (Chairmanship and Secretariat);
HM Inspectorate of Constabulary; DoT Civil Aviation Policy Directorate; DoT Principal Aviation Security Adviser; Ministry of Defence; Scottish Home and Health Department; Association of Chief Police Officers and ACPO (Scotland); Metropolitan Police; Aerodrome Owners Association; British Airports Authority (BAA); Heathrow Airport Limited; Joint Airports Committee of Local Authorities, and Manchester Airport.

No evidence there of any independent academic input, nor of any input from possible experts in the private side of security, from any of the consumers/passengers organisations, nor from the trades unions representing the people who work at airports and on the airlines. I would have thought that the presence of an independent inquisitive academic mind to question the reasoning behind much of the input to the working party would have been invaluable. Someone like Professor Wilkinson who is an internationally recognised expert on the subject of terrorism would have been an ideal member of such a body.

In fairness I do not know if the services of any such individuals were sought by the working party on an ad-hoc or co-opted basis, but even if so, this is wrong. *Such people should be there by right*, not as an afterthought. I admit to bias, being a trade-union sponsored MP by the Transport and General Workers Union, but it amazes me how little attention is paid to the input from workers and their representatives.

When the Select Committee visited Heathrow during our 1985/86 inquiry we were assured by BAA officials that security was very good. We then received representations from the trade unions that this was not the case and that there was much to be concerned about. We agreed to go back and to interview the unions but before we could, the El Al incident of the terrorist attempting to sacrifice his girlfriend occurred. Had it been any other airline than El Al the terrorist would probably have succeeded. When we did meet with the unions we were told by them that security had improved by 100 per cent since the El Al incident.

So much for the assurances given to the Committee on its earlier visit.

The Select Committee report in 1986 made 21 recommendations most of which the government accepted. However, there is a world of difference between acceptance and implementation, and monitoring such implementation. *Then Lockerbie happened.* The Select Committee went on to do another inquiry and a review of our earlier report, not into Lockerbie as such, but into airport security generally. This report formed the basis for the 1990 Marine and Aviation Security Act.

I had the very sad experience of meeting several families of Pan Am 103 victims, 4 Americans, 4 Europeans, who came to my home to discuss the tragedy with me. They will never get over it. Lockerbie has of course dominated any discussion on security in recent years. It has been suggested by some that if the Select Committee's earlier report had been taken more seriously Lockerbie might have been avoided. I honestly doubt that very much, but we shall never know. What I do believe is that there was a laxity in approach to security which led the Committee to believe that the accepted recommendations were never fully implemented. Even the wording of much of the government's response was somewhat unenthusiastic. *The Experts knew best.*

Your seminar has made me think that it would be a good thing if in 1993 the Committee was to do a follow up to the 1989 report and also examine the workings and effectiveness of the 1990 Marine and Aviation Security Act. I think and sincerely hope we would find the position to be much better.

There are some general points which I would like to make. Aviation is an international industry with most of the agreements being arrived at through the international civil aviation organisation based in Montreal. The pacemakers in the organisation tend to be the USA and Britain. The weakness in the system is that agreements tend to be on the basis of the lowest universally agreed standards rather than imposing the highest possible standards.

There really is no point in having isolated centres of excellence in an international system. There is a great need to strengthen co-operation nationally and internationally. One way, perhaps via the United Nations Security Council and General Assembly, would be to have some form of international security fund to assist countries who have difficulties in affording proper security measures and expensive equipment.

It is very important that commercial considerations and pressures be taken away entirely from the field of security. The government has always claimed that funding for security was not a problem, but I believe that it is and this is one specific area which could do with being examined closely.

Private security firms have been found wanting on occasions *vis-à-vis* the issue of security passes and their employment procedures. Much stiffer penalties should be imposed on all such breaches and such companies removed completely from aviation security. Security work is often boring and low paid. *Would anyone here fancy a job in security at an airport?* I do not think so! Ways and means of motivating, retaining, and valuing such staff must be found but it will not be easy.

It has been suggested that all security levels should be up to El Al standards but I do not believe this to be practical. El Al is a particularly high risk airline, but it is a small one, and to treat every airline the same would bring the world's airline traffic to a halt. There has to be a balance, which would obviously change if, heaven forbid, there were to be a spate of 'Lockerbies' all over the world, especially if one occurred in the USA where the feeling about the need for security is much less because they have not had any such disasters in their own country.

An example of a very secure airport is Belfast, but I am sure you will all agree that this is one example which could not be repeated at every other airport.

Technology alone will not solve the security problem. I am disappointed to admit that the select committee never really looked into technology to any great degree. There was not all that much available in any case. Barcode baggage tracking and reconciliation systems are a help. Thermal Neutron Activators (TNA) machines are allegedly another step forward but I wonder if they are not just window dressing in order to reassure the travelling public. I have yet to hear of a machine which can detect, without fail, all the variety of explosives available to terrorists. There may be such a machine but I doubt it. The Committee went to see a demonstration of the Condor machine but the computer equipment in it almost blew up. I understand that this machine is not 100 per cent successful either. One of the difficulties is that the authorities, for very good reasons, do not tell anyone what is happening. Even as a Select Committee with access to all sorts of highly confidential information we always had the feeling that there was more to it than what we were being told.

Britain has suffered from transport not having a sufficiently high political profile. The position of Secretary of State has been for someone on the road up or on the road out. We have had something like 10 secretaries of state in 13 years. No wonder the DoT leaves so much to be desired. Paul Channon was the one secretary of state for whom I had great respect. He was the only one, in my opinion, who was genuinely interested in transport but he was very unlucky with all the disasters which happened when he was in office.

The annual report of the Chief Inspector of Transport Security for 1991 states that 72 covert security tests were carried out in the UK. This is less than one-and-a-half per week. Such tests are the backbone of a good security system. Many more will have to be carried out in future or complacency will settle in yet again.

As security becomes more and more essential there is a good case for government providing more money for research and for training and educating people in the security field. This is still in its infancy and deserves encouragement.

I am very concerned about the effects of liberalisation. This will lead to cut-throat competition, extra flights, extra pressure on airline finances, on air traffic control and the availability of slots at busy airports. The cost of missing a slot is very great – especially for a 747 – so the temptation will be there for pilots to take a chance even if there is a doubt about some of the baggage.

What must be done immediately is to screen all transfer baggage, and substantial progress has been made in this direction. The next step is to screen *all* hold baggage, but this will take some time, especially in many foreign countries. Couriers, their baggage, and all rush cargo must be x-rayed.

In the longer term, all cargo must be screened. This may be where new technology would be most successful. If I wanted to blow an airliner out of the sky my best chance of success would be to do so using the cargo side of the industry, as I believe it to be the most vulnerable.

A couple of years ago it was estimated by the world's airlines that demand would grow by 250 per cent between 1989 and the year 2005. This will lead to greater scope and increased opportunities for terrorists and present ever greater challenges to the world's security systems.

The biggest dangers to security are human error, complacency and the 'it can't happen here' syndrome. Never ending vigilance has to be maintained at all times.

Sources of Terrorist Weaponry and Major Methods of Obtaining Weapons and Techniques

G. DAVIDSON SMITH

The threat of terrorism has not diminished. Co-operation and co-ordination amongst the intelligence and security communities, the military, government, business and academe remain of critical importance.

Terrorists utilize a broad range of weaponry – from the fundamental and expedient to the increasingly technical and sophisticated. The challenges presented by the scope of the modern terrorist arsenal demand an equally comprehensive response.

Terrorists can be expected to use scientific and technological developments in attempts to circumvent defence measures. The possibility that weapons of mass destruction may be used in future cannot be ruled out.

- In April 1992 *environmental activists* protesting against logging on Canada's West Coast drilled deep holes into timber trees, then inserted long spikes facing outward with the flat heads removed. If struck by a chain-saw or mill saw, the hidden spikes had the potential to explode outward with deadly force.[1]

- Also in 1992, in mid-western Canada the *Animal Liberation Front* claimed an arson attack against a commercial fish products distributor, in which two company vehicles were destroyed.[2] The improvised incendiary device consisted of three cans of BBQ lighter fluid, a bundle of wooden matches and an incense stick.

- It was revealed in November 1992 that *The Provisional Irish Republican Army* (PIRA) has an affinity for commercial electric

detonators manufactured in North America because of the efficiency and effectiveness of the detonators when used in PIRA's
improvised explosive devices.[3]

- Supporters of *foreign terrorist groups* have been purchasing
  commercial radar detectors and radio-controlled model toys in
  North America for the purpose of modifying the electronics for
  use in the remote-controlled detonation of bombs.[4]

- In January 1990 two Canadians were arrested in the United
  States when trying to purchase a Stinger anti-aircraft missile for
  delivery to PIRA.[5]

The purpose of citing these few examples is twofold. First, to underline that the terrorists of today utilise a broad range of weaponry – from
the fundamental and expedient to the increasingly technical and sophisticated. Second, to underscore the challenges presented by the scope of
the modern terrorist arsenal – challenges which demand an equally comprehensive response.

Co-operation and co-ordination amongst the intelligence and security
communities, the military, government, business and academe remain
of critical importance. The threat of terrorism has not diminished. One
should bear in mind that many of the incidents mentioned above involve
what has been described as the peaceable kingdom of Canada.[6]

Sources

In regard to the issue of sources, terrorist arsenals are largely based on
military weapons and equipment – automatic pistols, AK-47 type assault
rifles, machine-guns, grenades and grenade-launchers, even mortars –
that is, concealable, portable, robust weapons capable of high volumes
of fire, often used in company with explosive devices of a similar
nature.[7]

Because terrorists make wide use of conventional weapons, they tend
to keep abreast of the latest developments such as teflon-coated bullets
and improved sighting systems. For instance, some terrorist groups are
believed to have sought night-vision equipment, sniper-scopes and bul-
let-proof vests through North American sources.

Military stocks are frequently supplemented by commercially produced weapons, equipment and explosives. Many items designed for

police and security forces are equally suitable for use by terrorists. Explosives, detonators and fuses intended for commercial mining and construction purposes are ideal for improvised explosive devices, particularly car-bombs.[8]

Some well-organised groups have demonstrated a readiness and ability to employ sophisticated technologies, especially remote-controlled triggering devices for bombs – which are still the terrorist weapon of choice. A variety of initiating techniques have been introduced, including radar systems, x-rays, and time and barometric controls – so effective in attacks against aircraft.[9]

Ingenuity plays a large role as a source of terrorist weaponry. PIRA is undoubtedly a leader in the field, with its spectrum of home-made bombs, mortars and similar weapons; as well, PIRA has demonstrated its flexibility in the use of commercial fertilizer as an explosive ingredient.[10]

Although current trends suggest terrorist groups will continue to employ traditional methods in their attacks, the possibility that weapons of mass destruction may be used in the future cannot be ruled out. The decision may ultimately rest on an assessment of the potential gains and risks of using such weapons.[11]

Major Methods of Obtaining Weapons and Techniques

When considering major methods by which terrorists obtain weaponry and techniques, state-sponsorship comes readily to mind, especially in association with international terrorism. Over the past two decades many groups received training, weapons and technical expertise from the former Soviet Union and member states of the Warsaw Pact, as well as from North Korea, Syria, Libya, Iran, Iraq and Cuba.[12]

While changed circumstances in the former Soviet Union and Eastern Europe, as well as the outcome of the 1991 Gulf War, have placed constraints on the level of such support, some governments continue to pursue the practice. Iran provides support to Hizbollah in Lebanon, and has shipped weapons and equipment to training camps in the Sudan.[13] Contention remains over Hizbollah's role in the 1991 bombing of the Israeli Embassy in Buenos Aires, as well as possible Iranian complicity. Diplomatic bag privileges have been abused in the past for the covert movement of weapons, equipment and explosives to support terrorist activity.[14]

Despite disclaimers and the highly-publicised closures of former terrorist camps within its borders, Libya is believed to be providing at least covert funding assistance to some groups.[15] Although endeavouring to improve its image, Syria continues to permit training camps to be maintained in the Bekaa valley of South Lebanon.[16] Cuba and North Korea also provide safehaven to some terrorists.[17], and Pakistan has been teetering on the edge in regard to the nature and extent of its support for Sikh and Kashmiri militants in India.[18]

State-sponsorship of terrorism has encompassed money, weapons, equipment, and training. One of the more deadly involvements was the transfer of large amounts of Semtex explosive to terrorist groups, particularly by Libya. The Czech government has placed controls on the sale of Semtex, but considerable amounts are believed to be still available through other sources. The constraints on Semtex now serve to increase the attraction of C4, a standard plastic explosive found in many military arsenals.[19]

Difficulties in obtaining weapons supplies resulting from reduced state-support have been partly alleviated by stocks available in the newly emerging states on the periphery of the former Soviet Union. Weapons and equipment left behind by departing Soviet military are being used to equip new nationalist forces in Armenia, Azerbaijan and Tajikistan, for example, but some items are also finding their way on to the black market or into the hands of weapons merchants.[20] The sale of military arms and equipment offers an attractive method for some of the new cash-starved states to obtain foreign currency.

The changed circumstances in Afghanistan, where large stocks of weapons were supplied to both sides in the 1979–91 war provide another case in point. Of special concern are US Stinger and Soviet SAM anti-aircraft missiles still remaining in the country. It is feared that these weapons may enter the terrorist arms network, Current asking prices are estimated between $50,000 and $80,000 (US), depending on the type of missile.[21]

Commercial arms dealers are another source of weapons. In the past, some extremist groups, such as the Palestinian Liberation Organisation and the African National Congress, established dummy front companies to facilitate their purchases.[22] On the basis of earlier attempts by Hizbollah to move weapons and explosives into Europe concealed in food stuffs from the Middle East, container shipments to and from certain countries continue to be subject to monitoring by various security agencies.

Whenever possible, terrorists or their supporters will steal weapons and equipment from military or security forces, or from commercial establishments. A particular concern is the possible theft of tactical nuclear weapons or components or weapons-grade material from military sites in the former Soviet Union.[23]

Funding for the purchase of weapons and equipment can represent a major difficulty for terrorists.[24] Bank robbery is a common practice, even on the part of well-established groups. The Chilean Movement of the Revolutionary Left (MIR) collaborated with French criminals in the biggest-ever bank robbery in France at St. Nazaire. In January 1992 four members of MIR were arrested in Spain on charges of kidnapping in co-operation with the Madrid Commando of *Euzkadi ta Akatasuna* (ETA).[25]

In Canada, supporters of the Liberation Tigers of Tamil Eelam (LTTE) are known to indulge in extortion among members of the ethnic Tamil communities. Kidnapping of Tamils visiting Sri Lanka has also been reported, and Tamils have been implicated in immigration scams and the forging of passports and immigration control documents.[26]

Sikh extremists in several countries raise money to support terrorist violence in India through control of local temple funds.[27] PIRA obtains money in North America by 'legitimate' means through Irish social clubs which feature dances, public entertainment, and passing the hat in support of charitable causes.[28] Canadian authorities are unable to intervene because the money is claimed to be for charity – widows and orphans funds, etc. – and once the money has left the country it is impossible to trace.

Accusations have been made of terrorist involvement with narcotics trafficking. Undoubtedly such has been the practice in parts of Latin America, particularly in association with the *Sendero Luminoso* (Shining Path) in Peru. And certainly Pablo Escobar's Medellín Cartel remains the embodiment of narcoterrorism.[29] Yet terrorist groups have generally tried to avoid being identified with the trade, although involvement could increase in response to lessened support from state sponsors.

Many of the techniques of terrorism have been learned in camps provided by state-sponsors. Maritime and underwater specialists, for example, have been trained in Libya. Various camps in the Bekaa valley continue to provide the means to learn and practice the use of weapons, explosives and tactics – even hang-gliding, which was used to cross the Israeli border to attack a security post.[30]

Some training has been accomplished through linkages among terrorist groups, for instance ETA and PIRA are believed to have exchanged knowledge of explosive techniques. 'How-to' books, such as the *Anarchist Cookbook* are another source of basic instruction. Paladin Press, of *Soldier of Fortune* magazine fame, offers military training videos and related books which provide explicit instruction in the use of weapons, equipment and explosives.[31] Former soldiers, security and intelligence specialists, finding themselves less in demand in the changed global environment, are tending to be less discerning in terms of selecting clientele.

The official institutions of countries that sponsor terrorism have sometimes been involved in collecting scientific and technological information.[32] In the past, Iranian, Libyan and Iraqi students have attempted to obtain knowledge of scientific techniques which could be used in areas related to biological weapons and germ warfare. Although it seems improbable that a terrorist group will use such weapons of mass destruction to achieve its ends, some indicators suggest that this risk is growing with time.

Some terrorist groups have been very successful in making the transition to the computer age. Among other things, they have managed to intercept the conversations of authorities or to gain access to banking systems for the purpose of diverting or laundering funds. PIRA managed to hack into computers used by banks, credit card companies and other service agencies and used the ability to identify the residences of senior Royal Ulster Constabulary (RUC) officers.[33] In Canada, some of the issue groups, such as White Supremacists, are using computers as a means of communication and have developed highly complex coding systems.

Terrorists can be expected to continue using scientific and technological developments in attempts to circumvent defence measures and to carry out spectacular attacks to attract wide media attention.[34] As hard targets become still harder and security becomes tighter, terrorists will seek weaponry that avoids the necessity of penetrating perimeter defences and permits effective stand-off capabilities for conducting attacks.

NOTES

1. *The Province* (Vancouver, BC), 2 April 1992.
2. *Edmonton Journal*, 22 June 1992. See also 'Militant Activism and the Issue of Animal Rights', *Commentary Counter-Terrorism Security Intelligence* (hereafter CSIS), April 1992, No.21).
3. Reuter, 12 Nov. 1992.
4. CSIS, 27 Aug. 1990. See also: *Independent* (London), 7 Jan. 1990.
5. *Daily Telegraph* (London), 17 Jan. 1990.
6. G. Davidson Smith, *Combating Terrorism* (London: Routledge, 1990), p.32. See also *Toronto Star*, 28 Oct. 1992.
7. Christopher Dobson and Ronald Payne, *The Terrorists, Their Weapons, Leaders and Tactics*, rev. ed. (NY: Facts On File, 1982).
8. *Financial Times* (London), 21 Sept. 1990. See also Gannet News Service, 2 Oct 1989.

9. *The Terrorists* (note 7), pp.123–41. See also *Jane's Defence Weekly*, 12 May 1990.
10. *Sunday Telegraph* (London), 13 Jan. 1992. See also Edgar O'Ballance. *Terrorism in the 1980s* (London: Arms & Armour Press, 1989), pp.60–1.
11. Three Trips – 1. Terrorism: Forecast for the 1990s. *Commentary* (CSIS, Feb. 1992, No.17).
12. *Washington Times*, 25 July 1990, and 22 June 1990. See also *Los Angeles Times*, 12 Dec. 1989.
13. *San Francisco Chronicle*, 18 May 1992. See also *Middle East News Network*, 13 Dec. 1991.
14. *Combating Terrorism* (note 6), p.10. See also *New York Times*, 21 April 1991, and 18 March 1990; also, *Christian Science Monitor*, 4 Dec. 1986.
15. *Patterns of Global Terrorism: 1991* (Washington, DC: US Dept. of State, April 1992).
16. Ibid. See also *Washington Post*, 26 Jan. 1992.
17. *Patterns* (note 15). See also *Heritage Foundation Reports*, 25 Feb. 1988, and 4 June 1988.
18. *Reuter Library Report*, 19 Oct. 1992.
19. *Washington Times*, 22 June 1990. For a description of C4, see also Terrorist Weapons in the 80s. *Clandestine Tactics and Technology* 13/2 (1987).
20. Inter Press Service, 1 Oct. 1992. See also: *Agence France Presse*, 1 April 1992. For a description of weapons trafficking in Afghanistan, see *Soldier of Fortune*, Jan 1990.
21. *Financial Times* (London), 5 Sept. 1992. See also *Atlanta Journal and Constitution*, 13 Jan. 1992; and *Daily Telegraph* (London), 30 Oct. 1991.
22. *Sunday Times* (London), 22 July 1990.
23. *Periscope – Daily Defense News Capsules*, 6 July 1992.
24. FBIS-SOV-91-214 5 Nov. 1991, p.12.
25. *Intelligence Digest*, 5 June 1992.
26. *Toronto Star*, 11 March 1992.
27. *Sunday Telegraph* (London), 15 Dec, 1991.
28. *Chicago Tribune*, 23 March 1992. See also *Financial Times* (London), 7 Jan. 1992. Also, *Terrorism in the 1980s*, pp.59–60.
29. 'Terrorism and the Rule of Law: Dangerous Compromise in Colombia', *Commentary* (CSIS, Oct. 1991, No.13). See also *Montreal Gazette*, 21 April 1992; also *L'Express*, 13 March 1992.
30. FBIS-NES-87 30 Nov. 1987, p.16. See also *Jane's Defence Weekly*, 12 May 1990.
31. *Soldier of Fortune*, Oct. 1992.
32. Press Association Newsfile, 26 Jan. 1991. See also Associated Press, 24 Dec. 1990.
33. *Intelligence Newsletter*, 31 Jan. 1990.
34. *Defence Electronics*, Jan. 1990. Also, The Office of Technology Assessment, US Congress, has produced an interesting and informative examination: *Technology Against Terrorism, The Federal Effort*. (Washington , DC: US GPO, July 1991); and, *Technology Against Terrorism, Structuring Security*. (Washington, DC: US GPO, Jan. 1992).

Trends in Terrorist Weaponry

RICHARD CLUTTERBUCK

It has long been feasible for terrorists to acquire the means of using nuclear, biological and chemical weapons, but they are complex and hard to control and the threat to fire them may lack credibility. Amongst conventional weapons, hand-held missiles have brought about the greatest changes in terrorist tactics, but they are expensive so they need rich sponsors. Small arms have changed very little: the 1884 Maxim gun fired 13 rounds per second; so do the Armalite and the AK74. Submachine-guns have become smaller and lighter and about 150 models, some old but still serviceable, are available worldwide at very low cost. There is, however, no limit to ingenuity in improvising bombs, grenades and mortars, fired by readily available commercial radio-control and timing devices. These are likely to continue to cause most of the surprises as they are difficult to predict.

Nuclear, Biological and Chemical Weapons

A determined and sophisticated terrorist group could almost certainly acquire or assemble a nuclear, biological or chemical (NBC) weapon. This capability has been available for many years but has not thus far been used by terrorists, either for an attack or for a credible hoax (the only hoaxes so far have been quickly identified as such). Why was this so? And is the use, or threat of use, of nuclear weapons more likely in the future?

It is quite feasible – albeit requiring knowledge, skill and the necessary materials – to make a nuclear device in a laboratory. A US research student proved this some years ago. He did his experiments with a high sense of responsibility, in full co-operation with his supervisor, carrying out each individual process, but not in the order which would have produced a nuclear weapon. Some materials, including the nuclear materials, would not be impossible to acquire in small quantities, probably without detection, given a modicum of skill in planning, smuggling and deception.

Another means of acquiring a nuclear device was described by Frederick Forsyth in a fictional setting in his 1984 book *The Fourth Protocol*, in which a team in the Soviet Embassy, supplied by diplomatic bag from the USSR, assembled bit by bit the components and materials required, consignments being small and infrequent enough not to attract attention. Frederick Forsyth does the most meticulous research for his books and, though complicated, (and regardless of whether the USSR would ever have wished to have embarked on it), the project was almost certainly feasible.

The most likely scenario for terrorist use of a nuclear weapon would be to secrete it in one of several crates or containers packed with, say, automobile parts being consigned by sea to the target country. The device would be tracked and in due course fired by radio. When the ship arrived, the terrorist team would telephone a message, the gist of which would be: 'there is a nuclear bomb in the hold of a ship in one of your ports. Unless you agree to our demands by 12 noon tomorrow, we will detonate it.' They would, however, probably be reluctant to carry out the threat, since mass casualties are usually counterproductive. Operations such as blowing up the Air India flight over the Atlantic in 1985 (329 killed), or Pan Am 103 over Lockerbie in 1988 (270 killed) have been very rare, and have achieved nothing for their causes.

A nuclear explosion in a sea port would be even more counterproductive. If the government refused to comply with the demand, the terrorists would probably not detonate the bomb, and both sides would be aware of that. The operation would be flawed on three counts: control, complexity and credibility. Feasible as it is, it is harder to control the course of events, and much more complex to mount than, say, a kidnap, a threat to assassinate or a threat to bomb, using simple hand weapons or improvised grenades; so it is more likely to go wrong, and its perpetrators more likely to be detected; and the threat (of overkill) is less credible.

Biological warfare has been feasible for hundreds of years and was, for example, used in times of plague in the Middle Ages, by catapulting diseased corpses into besieged cities. But it has not been used in modern times, because the perpetrators would have even less control of the consequences.

Chemical weapons are also notoriously difficult to control, because gases drift with changes of wind and persist in unexpected places, whether they are fired in shells, dropped in bombs or, say, released by blowing up a storage tank of highly toxic liquid gas (one of the many regularly used in industry) up wind of a big city.

These arguments against terrorist use of NBC weapons will remain.

Their future use is neither more nor less likely than in the past. It remains feasible, however, so it is necessary still to maintain precautions against it, and contingency plans for crisis management in case the threat does materialise.

Of higher priority, however, is security against the more conventional terrorist weapons; guns, bombs, hand-held missile launchers and improved weapons, including mortars, grenades, mines and bombs.

Small Arms

The **Maxim** gun (1884), the first fully automatic machine-gun, fired 13 rounds per second (rps), and became the British **Vickers** machine-gun, one of the queens of the battlefield in the First World War. The US-made **Armalite** rifle (1960s), used in Vietnam and Northern Ireland, had not increased the rate of fire at all – still 13rps; its bullets were half the weight and, in some people's view, had half the stopping power. The same applied to the Kalashnikov **AK74** (1970s), a smaller calibre version of the **AK47** (1957) – perhaps the most widely used of all terrorist weapons.

An attempt at a quantum leap was made in the late 1980s, with the German-made Heckler & Koch **G11 Assault Rifle**. This fired a bullet a quarter of the weight of the Vickers .303in bullet. (The calibres were: Maxim/Vickers 7.62mm; Armalite 5.56mm; G11 4.7mm). The G11's normal rate of fire was slightly slower (10rps) but it had an ingenious loading and firing mechanism, using caseless ammunition (no cartridge to eject) which, as an alternative to normal automatic fire, offered a 3-round burst, which shot three rounds out of the barrel in one tenth of a second (a cyclic rate of 30rps) during the recoil – that is, before the firer felt any kick on his shoulder, so that these three rounds were very tightly grouped. The German Army, however, has not so far accepted the gun, so, after more than a century, the quantum leap in design, accuracy, rate of fire and reliability in the rifle and machine-gun field has still not taken place. Nor does it seem to be on the horizon.

In the submachine-gun field, since the reign of the **Tommy Gun** (1920s), the chief change has been in miniaturisation. The US-made Tommy Gun was 810mm (32in) long and weighed 5.37kg loaded. Steyr's 9mm **Tactical Machine Pistol** (TMP), undergoing user trials in 1993, has a high performance and is 282mm long; even smaller is the US Commercial **Ingram** (1950s), a favourite terrorist weapon, which is only 222mm (9in) long, and weighs 2.10kg loaded. Most submachine-guns fire 9mm ammunition, which has good stopping power at short range, the bullet being twice the weight with half the muzzle velocity of the 5.56mm Armalite bullet.

The all plastic pistol, with plastic bolts, springs and bullets, has been made, but has attracted few buyers. The plastic bullet is lethal at very short ranges (e.g., as in the hijacked aircraft), but has so far been rarely used except for training. Hijackers who want to smuggle a plastic gun on board an aircraft seem to prefer a replica weapon, which generally achieves the same object, and would get them into less trouble if it were found during their boarding search.

The chief problem from the anti-terrorist viewpoint is the proliferation of submachine-guns. *Jane's Infantry Weapons* lists 150 models, and they can be picked up worldwide at around $35.

Pistols, like rifles and machine-guns, have produced no fundamental advances. Ingenious ideas have appeared and faded away. Terrorists, criminals and policemen regularly turn back to the models essentially the same as those used in the Second World War, or even the First.

Shotguns (often adapted with shortened barrels for easier concealment) are devastatingly lethal up to 40 metres range, with a one metre spread. Pump action or fully automatic shotguns have a greatly increased rate of fire. Nevertheless, terrorists generally prefer smaller and more easily concealed weapons.

Hand Launched Missiles

Free flight missiles, such as the rocket-propelled grenade **RPG 7**, have been supplied to the IRA by Libya and other Arab countries formerly armed by the USSR. The IRA use them against buildings and armoured vehicles. They are usually effective only at short ranges, and if they strike a glancing blow, they are deflected without penetrating the target.

Guided surface-to-surface missiles (SSMs) are much more effective but also very expensive. For this reason, they are only likely to be found cost effective by terrorist movements with unlimited funds like the Palestinians and some other movements supported by oil states. The commonest current anti-tank models are the NATO **Milan** or its Russian equivalent, the **AT4**. The theoretical range is about 3000 metres but, against a small moving target, such as an armoured limousine, the maximum effective range is 2000 metres, with a flight time of about 12 seconds. The missile is wire-guided, so the operator has to pick a firing point from which he can see the road on which the target will be for the distance it is likely to drive in a little over 12 seconds – say about half a kilometre. Having launched the missile, he has only to keep the cross-hairs of his telescopic sight on the target, and the guidance system should ensure a hit. The launcher and missile will all fit into the boot of a car.

Developments are mainly in the guidance systems, including some models with heat-seeking or radar-guided missiles. These changes do not seem likely to make them much more attractive or cost effective for terrorists than the Milan or the AT4.

Surface-to-air missiles (SAMs) are much more attractive to terrorists and have been used to shoot down both civil airliners (e.g., in Rhodesia) and military helicopters (e.g., in Afghanistan). All modern marks are 'fire-and-forget' weapons – that is, – the guidance system is in the missile. The commonest systems are heat-seeking and radar. As with SSMs, current developments seem unlikely to change their appeal and effectiveness for terrorists, which are very high.

A US organisation tried in 1990 to provide **Stinger** SAMs to the IRA but this was intercepted by the Federal Bureau of Investigation. The USA did provide numerous Stingers to the Mujahedin in Afghanistan from 1986, and these were very effective against helicopters flown first by the USSR and then by the Najibullah government forces. Many remain in the hands of the guerrillas and, as they may not need them for what looks like being a prolonged civil war between them, they may be tempted to raise money by selling them to terrorist movements, perhaps at gift prices to Islamic fundamentalists in Algeria or to Bosnian Muslims.

Mortars

Mortars are valuable weapons for fighting in built-up areas. The small infantry mortar (51mm or 2in) is easily portable with a range of 800 metres. Terrorists, however, more often use improvised multiple mortars for attacking police stations, etc. On 7 February 1991 the IRA made a propaganda splash by landing two mortar bombs close to the British Prime Minister's London residence and Cabinet Room, Number 10 Downing Street, while a Cabinet meeting was in progress.

The normal design is to mount six or more steel pipes on the back of a truck or, as in the Downing Street attack, in a minivan with a gap cut in the roof. In this case, there was also a short delay incendiary device to set fire to the van immediately after the mortars were fired, to destroy forensic evidence.

A recent innovation is to use a photo-flash and slave unit to fire all the mortars at once. Professional photographers use these to fire simultaneous flashes to light the subject from different angles. They are fired by the slave unit when it is activated by the flash when he clicks the camera. The terrorist aims his flash gun at his slave unit from a safe distance to fire the mortars.

Grenades

Nearly all terrorist grenades are improvised. The simplest is the **nail bomb**, used by the IRA for the past 20 years; it is made from a few sticks of commercial explosive bound in tape with a handful of 6in nails, with a 3 or 4-second length of safety fuse.

A more sophisticated IRA weapon is the **drogue grenade**, designed to penetrate army or police armoured landrovers, most commonly by throwing it from a window on to the roof of the vehicle. The charge is plastic explosive packed into a beer can, shaped by a metal cone at the front end to give it the armour-piercing power of a hollow charge. The detonator is embedded in the plastic, and is fired by a rim cartridge. The firing pin is a heavy bolt with a chisel end, which fires the rim cartridge on impact. This bolt, in the safe position, is held by a detent at the top of a tube. The tube is fixed into a wooden block plugged tightly into the top of the can. To use the grenade, the operator first removes a safety pin, but he still clutches a lever lying against the tube, which acts like the lever of a conventional First or Second World War grenade (the 'Mills Bomb'): when released, the lever flies up on a spring and extracts the detent. The firing bolt is now loose, held only by a light spring, as the grenade falls towards its target. When it strikes, the bolt crushes the light spring and falls heavily onto the rim cartridge, firing it. To help the grenade to fly straight, nose first, the firing lever also releases a light plastic drogue, which flies behind the grenade as it falls.

The drogue grenade can also be throw horizontally, but it is then less likely to hit its target squarely. It is most effective when dropped or thrown from above.

A recent alternative is the **limpet bomb**, a few sticks of explosive in a plastic lunch box, fired by a 3-second electronic microswitch, and fitted with a powerful magnet. Typically, this is carried by the pillion rider on a motor-cycle, who places it on the roof of the target car or landrover as he overtakes it in the street. This is an adaptation of the more commonly used bomb fixed magnetically under a car with a delay or tilt fuse (see below).

Road Mines

To catch passing patrols in rural areas, **road mines**, also, are almost always improvised, comprising very large charges of home-made bulk explosive (e.g., made from fertilizer and diesel fuel), with a priming charge of a stick or two of commercial explosive and an electric detonator. They are placed under culverts or in parked vehicles by the roadside. In the last two assassination attempts by the Red Army Faction in Germany, the charge was on a parked bicycle. The mine is usually fired by an electric cable or radio signal from an observation post providing a covered getaway. Alternatively, it can be fired by a magnetic or photo-electric device (as in the two German bicycle bombs), operated by the target vehicle as it passes, but the device must be made live by a radio signal as the target vehicle approaches.

There are many ingenious alternatives, limited only by the imagination of the designer. One method used by the IRA was to fix a large square laminated 'placard' on the side of a parked van containing the charge. The placard comprised two metal sheets separated by a layer of insulating material a few millimetres thick. The metal sheets were connected to the two ends of a firing circuit, which was instantaneously closed by a rifle bullet fired from 200 yards away, as the target vehicle passed by.

Factory-made military **anti-tank mines** are often used on dirt roads where they can be easily dug in and concealed. They are fired by pressure from a wheel or track, usually of 150kg or more, to prevent them being prematurely exploded by an animal or pedestrian. The Arabs use a lot of these.

Car and Truck Bombs

Car and truck bombs have been used by terrorists worldwide, ever since a truck with a huge charge and a delay fuse was driven into the inner courtyard of the King David Hotel at Jerusalem by Jewish terrorists on 22 July 1946. Currently, those used by Arabs, the IRA and ETA usually contain huge bulk charges of improvised explosives, fired by a radio signal or with a timing device. Islamic fundamentalists seeking martyrdom have sometimes driven them into the heart of a target (e.g., the US Marine Corps base at Beirut airport in 1983), when they have been fired either by the drivers or, more often, by remote radio control, in case the driver is shot by guards. Early 1993 saw increasing use of giant truck bombs containing a ton or more of explosives in city centres, for example in New York, London and Protestant town centres in Northern Ireland. The one in the New York World Trade Center killed 6 people and wounded over 1000.

Anti-personnel mines or **booby traps** are frequently used by terrorists, in the vicinity of culvert or roadside mines or of car or truck bombs, to inflict casualties on police or ambulance personnel coming to rescue the wounded. These may either be buried with light pressure switches, or fired by tripwires across the approaches. Booby traps, fired by a variety of methods – pull or pressure switches or remote control –

are used to catch police investigating a suspiciously parked vehicle, or answering a call to a reported 'crime'. Firemen may also be targets of booby traps or of gunmen lying in ambush.

Another kind of car bomb is that designed to kill the driver of a car when he comes to drive it away – or his passenger. These may be booby traps fired by opening the door, switching on the ignition or depressing the clutch pedal. More commonly, they they are **under car bombs** fixed by a magnet to the chassis under the driver's or passenger's seat, or inside the mudguard (wing). These are usually operated by a **tilt fuse**; this is a small glass or plastic tube, such as is used for packaging medical tablets; the bottom end is closed and contains liquid mercury; at the open end, incorporated in the stopper, are the ends of two wires which are terminals of an electric firing circuit. When the tube is jerked or tilted, the mercury moves up and closes the circuit. If the terrorist desires a strong impulse or jerk to fire it, he will tilt the tube steeply. If it is tilted more gently, it will be more sensitive. So the circuit is closed when the car accelerates or brakes or goes over a bump.

To avoid risk to the terrorist from accidentally jerking the tube, it is customary to include a timing device (electronic or clockwork) so that the circuit does not become live until, say, 20 minutes after the terrorist has set the bomb under the car, to enable him to get clear. A bomb like this can be switched on and slipped under a parked car in a few seconds.

A Growing Use of Electronics in Firing Bombs

Terrorists have made increasing use of radio and electronic devices readily available in the shops: notably the simple mechanisms used for remote control of model aircraft and boats; and the timing devices used to set a video-recorder to record a television programme at a precise time, accurate to one second, many days or weeks ahead. Some timers can be set up to a year in advance.

A precise delay fuse was set by an IRA man who booked a room in the Grand Hotel at Brighton in October 1984, three weeks before the Conservative Party Conference. It was timed to fire a large bomb which he concealed behind a panel in the bathroom in a room above the suites in which the Prime Minister and her Cabinet would be sleeping in the early hours of the morning. It did not kill any Cabinet ministers, though it did kill five other people. The man who attempted this assassination was later caught and convicted after another bomb was found in a London hotel, and plans were captured to set more in London and in 12 seaside resorts, presumably intended to deter foreign tourists from visiting Britain.

Bombs in Aircraft

The Lockerbie disaster in December 1988 proved that a charge of less than 1lb of Semtex explosive, if located close to the fuselage in an unreinforced cargo hold, can destroy an aircraft in flight with the loss of hundreds of lives.

Such bombs are usually fitted with a timing device imposing a delay of at least 30 minutes after take-off, and more often several hours, to ensure that the aircraft reaches its cruising altitude and, where possible, that the bomb explodes over the sea. This happened to the Air India flight which exploded over the Atlantic Ocean, killing 329 people in 1985 so that, unlike the bomb in Pan Am 103 over Lockerbie, it left no forensic evidence.

An alternative, to allow for an unexpected delay in take-off, is to use a barometric device which activates at a little below cruising altitude. If the flight plan includes a substantial time over the sea, the barometric device will probably be used to trip a timing device rather to fire the bomb direct. The fact that the Lockerbie bomb exploded before the aircraft reached the coast suggests that there was no barometric device, and this appears to be borne out by the forensic evidence.

Bombs in aircraft may also be fired by radio signals, but this is less common.

The commonest means of getting a bomb on board an aircraft has been in passengers' checked baggage, which has in the past been inadequately searched. Reconciliation of passengers and their baggage, to ensure that the owner of every bag is on board before take-off, is probably more effective than searching, since suicide bombers are, in fact, rare. The subject of aviation security, including baggage reconciliation, is discussed at some length elsewhere in this volume.

Conclusions

Most of the surprises in terrorist weapons in recent years have been the result of ingenious ideas for improvisation. The exception has been the use of radio control and of precise delay switches like those in videorecorders. These are easily obtained and simple to use. Terrorists generally prefer simple weapons, such as bombs, automatic pistols, submachine-guns and assault rifles, and avoid high tech weapons which are more likely to go wrong. There has in any case been little fundamental change in small arms, which long ago reached a degree of accuracy superior to that of the most skilled user. There is again a notable exception – the handheld guided surface-to-air missile. Most of those used so far have been of designs of at least five years old, but if these weapons improve, and especially if they become more simple, terrorists are likely to take advantage of these improvements, since helicopters and low-flying aircraft are amongst their most feared enemies. Effective SAMs are, however, very expensive, and terrorists without wealthy backers may think it more cost effective to have hundreds or even thousands of small arms for the same price.

It has been feasible for many years for terrorists to use nuclear, biological and chemical weapons, but they have not done so. The reasons probably lie in the difficulty of making the threat credible and of controlling the effects; also the complexity of the operation in comparison with the use of small arms and improvised mortars, grenades and bombs.

The most effective terrorist surprises have usually been achieved with improvised weapons in which there is no limit to imagination in design. This trend is certainly the likeliest to continue.

Select Bibliography

Adams, James, *The Financing of Terror* (London: New English Library, 1986), 293pp.

Alexander, Yonah, 'Super Terrorism' in Y. Alexander and J.M. Gleason, (eds.), *Terrorism: Behavioral Perspectives* (NY: Pergamon Press, 1980), pp.343–62.

—— 'Terrorism and High-Technology Weapons' in Y. Alexander and L. Z. Freedman (eds.), *Perspectives on Terrorism* (Wilmington, DE: Scholarly Resources, 1983), pp.225–40.

Alexander, Yonah, David Carlton and Paul Wilkinson, *Terrorism: Theory and Practice* (Boulder, CO, Westview Press, 1978).

Alexander, Yonah and Robert A Kilmarx, *Political Terrorism and Business: The Threat and Response* (NY: Praeger, 1979).

Alexander, Yonah and Alan O'Day, *The Irish Experience* (Aldershot, Dartmouth Press, 1991).

Annals of the American Academy of Political and Social Science, Special ed. on 'Guerrilla, Sabotage Organizations, Operations, Motivations, Escalation.' May 1962.

Aron, Raymond, *Peace and War* (London: Weidenfeld & Nicolson, 1966).

Backes, Uwe, *Politischer Extremismus in Demokratischen Verfassungstaaten* (Opladen: Westdeutsher Verlag, 1989).

Beaufre, André, *La Guerre Revolutionaire: Les Formes Nouvelles de la Guerre* (Paris: Fayard, 1972).

Beckwith, Charles A., and Donald Knox, *Delta Force: The Inside Story of America's Super-Secret Counterterrorist Unit* (London: Fontana, 1985).

Berard, Stanley P., 'Nuclear Terrorism: More Myth than Reality', [US] *Air University Review* 36/3 (July 1985), pp.30–6

Beres, Louis Rene, 'International terrorism and World Order' in A.R. Norton and M.H. Greenberg (eds.), *Studies in Nuclear Terrorism* (Boston, MA: G.K. Hall, 1979), pp.360–78.

—— *Terrorism and Global Security: The Nuclear Threat.* (Boulder, CO: Westview Press, 1979), 161pp.

—— *Apocalypse: Nuclear Catastrophe in World Politics.* (Chicago, IL: Univ. of Chicago Press, 1980).

Blair, Bruce G. and Garry D. Brewer, 'the Terrorist Threat to World Nuclear Programs', *Journal of Conflict Resolution* 21/3 (Sept. 1977), pp.379–403.

Boskey, Bennett and Mason Willrich (eds.), *Nuclear Proliferation: Prospects for Control* (NY: Dunellen, 1970).

Brenchley, Frank, *Living with Terrorism: The Problem of Air Piracy*. London, Conflict Studies, No.184 (1985).

Brodie, Thomas G., *Bombs and Bombings: A Handbook to Detection, Disposal and Investigation for Police and Fire Departments* (Springfield, IL: C.C. Thomas, 1975).

Carlton, David and Carlo Schaerf (eds.), *International Terrorism and World Security* (London: Croom Helm, 1975).

—— *Arms Control and Technological Innovation* (London: Croom Helm, 1977).

—— *The Hazards of the International Energy Crisis* (London: Macmillan, 1982).

Chaliand, Gérard, *Revolution in the Third World: Myths and Prospects* (Hassocks: The Harvester Press, 1977).

—— *Terrorismes et guerrillas: techniques actuelles de la violence* (Paris: Flammarion, 1985).

Chase, L. J. (ed.), *Bomb Threats, Bombings and Civil Disturbances: A Guide for Facility Protection* (Cornvallis, OR: Continuing Education Publications, 1971).

Clark, Richard, C., *Technological Terrorism* (Old Greenwich, CT: Devin-Adair, 1980), 220pp.

Clery, Daniel, 'Can we stop another Lockerbie?' *New Scientist*, 27 Feb. 1993, pp.21–3.

Clutterbuck, Richard, (ed.) *The Future of Political Violence* (London: Macmillan, 1986).

Clutterbuck, Richard *Terrorism and Guerrilla Warfare* (London, Routledge, 1990).

—— *Terrorism. Drugs and Crime in Europe After 1992* (London, Routledge, 1990).

Clyne, P., *An Anatomy of Skyjacking* (London: Abelard-Shuman, 1973).

Cohen, Bernard L., 'The Potentialities of Terrorism', *Bulletin of the Atomic Scientists* 32 (June 1976), pp.34–5.

Conrad, Thomas M., and L. Douglas DeNike, 'Radioactive Malevolence', *Bulletin of the Atomic Scientists* 30 (Feb. 1974), pp.16–20.

Council of Europe, *Defence of Democracy Against Terrorism in Europe* (Strasbourg: Council of Europe, 1981).

Crelinsten, Ronald D., 'Terrorism, Counter-Terrorism and Democracy: The Assessment of National Security Threats', *Terrorism and Political Violence* 1/2 (April 1989), pp.242–69.

Cross, Richard F., 'Bomb Protection Plans for Banks', *Bankers Magazine* 154 (Summer 1971), pp.83–8.

David, B. 'The Capability and Motivation of Terrorist Organizations to Use Mass-Destruction Weapons' in A. Merari (ed.), *On Terrorism and Combating Terrorism* (Frederick, MD: Univ. Publications of America, 1985), pp.145–56.

142   TECHNOLOGY AND TERRORISM

Day, David, *The Eco Wars: A Layman's Guide to the Ecology Movement* (London: Harrap, 1989).

Determination by Sheriff Principal John S. Mowat QC in the Fatal Accident Inquiry relating to the Lockerbie Air Disaster (Sheriff Court House, Airdrie, 1991).

Dewar, Michael, *The British Army in Northern Ireland* (London: Arms & Armour Press, 1985).

—— *Weapons and Equipment of Counter-Terrorism* (London: Arms & Armour Press, 1987).

Dillon, Martin, *The Dirty War* (London: Arrow Books, 1990).

Dobson, Chris and Ronald Payne, *Weapons of Terror* (London: Macmillan, 1979).

Dodd, Norman L., 'Send for Felix', [US] *Military Review* 58/3 (March 1978), pp.46–55. [See book by Patrick.]

Elliott-Bateman, M. (ed.), *The Fourth Dimension of Warfare* (Manchester: Manchester UP, 1970).

—— J. Ellis and T. Bowden, *Revolt to Revolution: Studies in the 19th and 20th Century European Experience* (Manchester: Manchester UP, 1974).

Emerson, Steven and Brian Duffy, *The Fall of Pan Am 103* (London, Futura, 1990).

Evans, Alona E., *Aerial Hijacking* (Springfield, IL: ? publisher 1974).

Feld, Bernard T. 'The Menace of Fission Power Economy'. *Science and Public Affairs* 30 (April 1974), pp.32–4.

—— 'Nuclear Violence at the Non-Governmental level', in D. Carlton and C. Schaerf (eds.), *Contemporary Terror* (London: Macmillan, 1981), pp.37–49.

Flood, Michael, 'Nuclear Sabotage'. *Bulletin of the Atomic Scientists* 32 (Oct. 1976), pp.29–38; p.33 (Jan. 1977).

Fowler, William, *An Agenda for Quantitative Research on Terrorism* (Santa Monica, CA: RAND Corp., 1980).

—— *Terrorism Data Bases: A Comparison of Missions, Methods and Systems* (Santa Monica, CA: RAND Corp., 1981).

Greenberg, M.H. and S. Althoff (eds.), *Preventing Nuclear Theft – Guidelines for Industry and Government* (NY: Praeger, 1972).

Greenwood, Ted, 'Discouraging Nuclear Proliferation in the Next Decade and Beyond: Non-State Entities', in A.R. Norton and M.H. Greenberg (eds.), *Studies in Nuclear Terrorism* (Boston, MA: G.K. Hall, 1979), pp.139–46.

Gross, Feliks, *The Seizure of Political Power in a Century of Revolutions* (NY: New Philosophical Library, 1958).

—— *The Revolutionary Party: Essays in the Sociology of Politics* (Westport, CT: Greenwood Press, 1974).

Gutteridge, William (ed.), *The New Terrorism* (London, Mansell Publishing, 1986).

Hamilton, Peter, *Espionage, Terrorism and Subversion in an Industrial Society* (Leatherhead: Peter Helms, 1979).

Harvey, A.D., 'The Pistol as Assassination Weapon: A Case of Technological Lag', *Terrorism and Political Violence* 3/2 (Summer 1991), pp.92–8.

Hearnden, Keith, *A Handbook of Computer Security* (London: Kogan Page, 1987).

Heilbrunn, Otto, *Partisan Warfare* (NY: Praeger, 1962).

Hewitt, Christopher, *The Effectiveness of Anti-Terrorist Policies* (NY: UP of America, 1984).

Hirsch, D., S. Murphy and B. Ramberg, 'Protecting Reactors from Terrorists', *Bulletin of the Atomic Scientists* 42/3 (1986), pp.22–5.

Hoffman, Bruce, 'Rightwing terrorism in Europe', *Conflict* 5/3 (Autumn 1984), pp.185–210.

—— 'Recent trends in Palestinian terrorism' (Santa Monica, CA: RAND Corp., 1985).

—— 'The Plight of the Phoenix: the PLO since Lebanon', *Conflict Quarterly* 4/1 (Spring 1985), pp.5–17.

—— *et al.*, 'A reassessment of potential adversaries to US nuclear programs' (Santa Monica, RAND Corp., 1986).

—— 'Terrorism in the US and the potential threat to nuclear facilities' (Santa Monica, RAND Corp., 1986).

Holsti, Kalevi J., *Peace and War: Armed Conflicts and International Order 1648–1989* (Cambridge: CUP, 1991).

Holton, Gerald, 'Reflections on Modern Terrorism', *Terrorism* 1 (1978), pp.265–76.

Hooper, Richard R., 'The Covert Use of Chemical and Biological Warfare Against United States Strategic Forces', *Military Medicine* 148/12 (Dec. 1983), pp.901–12.

Howard, Michael, *War in European History* (Oxford: OUP, 1976).

—— *The Causes of Wars and Other Essays* (London: Temple Smith, 1983).

Huntley, Bob, *Bomb Squad* (London: W.H. Allen, 1977).

Hutchinson, Martha C., 'Defining Future Threats: Terrorists and Nuclear Proliferation' in Y. Alexander and S.M. Finger (eds.), *Terrorism: Interdisciplinary Perspectives* (NY: John Jay Press, 1977), pp.298–316.

—— 'Defining Future Threat: Terrorists and Nuclear Proliferation' in A.R. Norton and M.H. Greenberg (eds.), *Studies in Nuclear Terrorism* (Boston, MA.: G.K. Hall, 1979), pp.147–63.

Imai, Ryukichi, *Nuclear Safeguards* Adelphi Papers, No.86 (London: IISS, 1973).

Jenkins, Brian, *International Terrorism: A New Kind of Warfare* (Santa Monica, CA: RAND Corp., 1974).

—— 'High Technology Terrorism and Surrogate War: The Impact of New Technology on Low-Level Violence', in G. Kemp, R.L. Pfaltzgraff and U. Raanan (eds.), *The Other Arms Race: New Technologies and Non-Nuclear Conflict* (Lexington, MA: Lexington Books, 1975), pp.91–108.

—— 'High Technology Terrorism and Surrogate War: The Impact of New Technology on Low-Level Violence' (Santa Monica, CA: RAND Corp., 1975).

—— *Will Terrorists Go Nuclear?* (Santa Monica, CA: RAND Corp., 1975).

—— *Combating Terrorism: Some Policy Implications* (Santa Monica, CA: RAND Corp., 1981).

—— *New Modes of Conflict*, (Santa Monica, CA: RAND Corp., 1983).

—— *Terrorism and Personal Protection*, (Boston, MA: Butterworth, 1985).

Johnson, Chalmers, *Autopsy on People's War* (Berkeley CA: Univ. of California Press, 1973).

Jones, R.V., *Reflections on Intelligence* (London: Heinemann, 1989).

Jones, J.M. and T.W. Hoover, 'Department of Energy (DOE) Transportation System for Nuclear Materials and the Role of State Law Enforcement Agencies, in J.S. Jackson (ed.) *Carnahan Conference on crime Countermeasures* (Lexington, KY: Ores Publications, 1978). 5pp.

Kennedy, Paul, *Preparing for the Twenty-First Century* (London, Harper-Collins, 1993).

Kupperman, Robert H., and D.M. Trent, *Terrorism: Threat, Reality and Response* (Stanford, CA: Hoover Inst., 1979).

Laffey, J.K., 'Nuclear Terrorism', *Journal of Security Administration* 5/1 (1982). pp.57–74.

Lakos, Amos, *International Terrorism: A Bibliography* (Boulder, CO: Westview Press, 1986).

Laqueur, Walter, *Terrorism* (London: Weidenfeld & Nicolson and Boston, MA: Little, Brown, 1977), 385pp.

Leachman, Robert B., and P. Althoff, (eds.), *Preventing Nuclear Theft – Guidelines for Industry and Government* (NY: Praeger, 1972),408pp.

Lenz, Robert R., *Explosives and Bomb Disposal Guide* (Springfield, IL: C.C. Thomas, 1973).

Livingstone, Neil C., 'Is Terrorism Effective?' *International Security Review* 6 (Fall 1981), pp.387–409.

—— *The War Against Terrorism* (Lexington, MA: Lexington Books, 1982).

Lodge, Juliet (ed.), *The Threat of Terrorism* (London: Wheatsheaf and Boulder, CO: Westview Press, 1987).

Lyons, H.A., 'Terrorist Bombings and the Psychological Sequelae', *Journal of the British Medical Association* 67/1 (Jan. 1974), pp.15–19.

Macdonald, Peter G., *Stopping the Clock: Bomb Disposal in the World of Terrorism* (London: Hale, 1977).

Mackenzie-Orr, Brigadier M.H., 'Aviation Security in an Age of Terrorism', *Flight Safety Foundation*, 41st IASS, Sydney, 1988, pp.338–43.

Mallin, Jay, (ed.) *Terror and Urban Guerrillas: A Study of Tactics and Documents* (Coral Gables, FLA: Univ. of Miami Press, 1971).

Mengel, R. William, 'Terrorism and New Technologies of Destruction: An Overview of the Potential Risk' in A.R. Norton and M.H. Greenberg, (eds.), *Studies in Nuclear Terrorism* (Boston, MA: G.K. Hall, 1979). pp.189–245.

Mickolus, Edward F., 'What Constitutes State Support to Terrorists?' *Terrorism and Political Violence* 1/3 (July 1989), pp.287–93.

Morgan, F., 'Judgement in Safeguards Activities' in R.B. Leachman and R. Althoff (eds.), *Preventing Nuclear Theft: Guidelines for Industry and Government* (NY: Praeger, 1972), 15pp.

Morris, Bruce L., 'Structural Damage to Building Frames From Accidental or Terrorist Explosions'. Paper presented to the Explosives Safety Seminar, held 24–26 Aug. 1982, Norfolk, Virginia, Vol.1.

Moss, David, *The Politics of Left-Wing Violence in Italy, 1969–85* (Basingstoke, Hants: Macmillan, 1989).

Moss, Robert, *Urban Guerrilla Warfare* (London: IISS, 1971), *Adelphi Papers* [Note: Minimanual of the Urban Guerrilla by Carlos Marighella is printed in the Appendix.]

—— *The Collapse of Democracy* (London: Abacus, 1977).

Most, John, *Revolutionare Kriegswissenschaft* and *The Beast of Property* (NY, Kraus Reprint, 1983).

Motley, J.B., 'Terrorist Warfare: A Reassessment', *Military Review* 65/6 (June 1985), pp.45–57.

Northedge, Fred S. (ed.), *The Use of Force in International Relations* (London, Faber, 1974).

Norton, Augustus R., 'Nuclear Terrorism and the Middle East' in A.R. Norton and M.H. Greenberg (eds.), *Studies in Nuclear Terrorism* (Boston, MA: G.K. Hall, 1979), pp.278–89.

—— and Martin H. Greenberg (eds.), *Studies in Nuclear Terrorism* (Boston, MA: G.K. Hall, 1979). 465pp.

O'Neill, B.E., W.R. Heaton, and D.J. Alberts, *Insurgency in the Modern World* (Boulder, CO: Westview Press, 1980).

Patrick, Lt.-Col. Derrick, *Fetch Felix: The Fight Against the Ulster Bombers 1976–77* (London: Hamish Hamilton, 1981).

Pike, Earl A., *Protection Against Bombs and Incendiaries: For Business, Industrial and Educational Institutions* (Springfield, IL: C.C. Thomas, 1973).

Powell, William, *The Anarchist Cookbook* (NY: Lyle Stewart, 1971).

Qualter, T.H., *Propaganda and Psychological Warfare* (NY, Random House, 1962).

Rapoport, David (ed.), *Inside Terrorist Organizations* (London: Frank Cass, 1989).

Reich, Walter (ed.), *Origins of Terrorism*, (Cambridge, UK: CUP, 1990).

Report of the President's Commission on Aviation Security and Terrorism (Washington DC: US GPO, 1990).

Reports of the House of Commons Select Committee on Transport on Aviation Security, 1986 and 1989.

Revell, Oliver B., 'Structure of Counterterrorism Planning and Operations in the United States', *Terrorism* 14/3 (July–Sept. 1991), pp.135–144.

Roetter, Charles, *Psychological Warfare* (London: Faber, 1974).

Rogers, N.F., 'Defuse Bomb Threats', *Security Management* 27 (Oct. 1983), pp.32–36.

St. John, Peter, *Air Piracy, Airport Security and International Terrorism: Winning the War against Hijackers* (NY: Quorum Books, 1991).

Salamanca, Beth A., 'Vehicle Bombs: Deaths on Wheels' in N.C. Livingstone and T.E. Arnold (eds.), *Fighting Back: Winning the War Against Terrorism* (Lexington, MA: Lexington Books, 1985), pp.35–48.

Salamon, Benjamin, 'Thinking About Nuclear Terrorism', *International Security* 6/4 (Spring 1982), pp.61–77.

Sanders, Benjamin, *Safeguards Against Nuclear Proliferation* (Cambridge, MA: MIT Press, 1975). 114pp.

Schelling, Thomas C., 'Can Nuclear Terrorism Be Neutralized?' in B. Netanyahu (ed.), *International Terrorism: Challenge and Response* (New Brunswick, NJ: Transaction Books, 1981), pp.155–9.

—— 'Thinking About Nuclear Terrorism'. *International Security* 6/4 (Spring 1982), pp.61–77.

Schmid, Alex P., and Albert J. Jongman, *et al.*, *Political Terrorism: A New Guide to Actors, Authors, Concepts, Data Bases, Theories, and Literature* (Amsterdam: North-Holland Publishing, 1988), 700pp.

Schultz, Richard, Study of the selective use of political terrorism in process of revolutionary warfare: NLF of South Vietnam, *International Behavioral Scientist* 8/2 pp.43–77.

Smith, G. Davidson, 'Military Options in Response to State-Sponsored Terrorism', *Terrorism and Political Violence* 1/3 (July 1989), pp.294–323.

—— *Combating Terrorism* (London, Routledge, 1990).

Stoffel, John, *Explosives and Homemade Bombs* (Springfield, IL: C.C. Thomas, 1973).

Styles, George, 'The Car Bomb', *Journal of the Forensic Science Society* 15 (April 1975), pp.93–7.

—— 'Bombs and Bomb Beaters', *International Defense Review* 9 (Oct. 1976), pp.817–19.

—— 'Defeating the Terrorist Bomber', *International Defense Review* 10 (Feb. 1977), pp.121–2.

—— 'Terrorist Bombings', *Executive Risk Assessment* 1/9 (1979), pp.1–6.

Thompson, Sir Robert, *Revolutionary War in World Strategy, 1945–69* (London: Secker & Warburg, 1970).

Thornton, T.P., 'Terror as a Weapon of Political Agitation' in H. Eckstein (ed.), *Internal War* (NY: Free Press, 1964).

Truby, J.D., 'Improvised/Modified small arms used by terrorists', Gaithersburg, Maryland, Int'l Assoc. of Chiefs of Police.

United Nations Office of Public Information, 'Terrorist Acts Against UN Missions', *UN Monthly Chronicle* 8 (Nov. 1971), pp.61–70.

US Congress, House Committee on the Armed Services Subcommittee on Investigations. *Thefts and Losses of Military Weapons, Ammunition and Explosives Report.* 94th Congress, 2nd Sess., (Washington, DC: US GPO, 1976).

US Congress, House Committee on Foreign Affairs, Subcommittee on International Operations, Hearing on International Operations on Europe and the Middle East: *The US Embassy Bombing in Beirut* (Washington, DC: US GPO, 1983).

US Congress, Senate Committee on the Judiciary, Subcommittee to Investigate the Administration of the Internal Security Act and Other Internal Security, *Terrorist Activity Part 7: Terrorist Bombings – Hearings.* 94th Congress, 1st Sess. (Washington, DC: US GPO, 1975).

US Congress, Senate Committee on the Judiciary, 94th Congress, 1st Sess., *Terrorist Activity, Hearings, Part 7: Terrorist Bombings and Law Enforcement Intelligence* (Washington, DC: US GPO, 1976).

US Congress, Office of Technology Assessment (OTA) *Technology Against Terrorism: The Federal Effort* (Washington, DC: US GPO, 1991).

US Federal Aviation Administration, Civil Aviation Security Service *Explosives Aboard Aircraft* (1949–79) (Washington, DC: US FAA, 1979).

US Federal Bureau of Investigation *Bomb Summary, 1984* (Washington, DC: US GPO, 1985).

Verfassungsungsschutz-bericht 1992 (Bonn, Bundesminister Innern, 1992).

148   TECHNOLOGY AND TERRORISM

Walter, E.V., *Terror and Resistance* (NY: OUP, 1969).

Wilkinson, Paul, *Political Terrorism* (Basingstoke, Hants, Macmillan, 1974).

Wilkinson, Paul (ed.), *British Perspectives on Terrorism*, (London: Allen & Unwin, 1981).

Wilkinson, Paul, 'Navies in a Terrorist World' in John Moore (ed.), *Jane's Naval Review* (1986), pp.166–76.

Wilkinson, Paul, *Terrorism and the Liberal State*, 2nd ed. (Basingstoke, Hants: Macmillan and NY: NY UP, 1986).

Wilkinson, Paul, *The Lessons of Lockerbie*, Conflict Study No.226 (London: Research Institute for the Study of Conflict and Terrorism, 1989).

Wilkinson, Paul, 'Designing Effective National Aviation Security Systems', *Terrorism and Political Violence* 1/3 (July 1989), pp.378–90.

Wilkinson, Paul, 'International Terrorism: New Risks to World Order' in John Baylis and N.J. Rengger (eds.), *Dilemmas of World Politics* (Oxford: Clarendon Press, 1992), pp.228–60.

Wilkinson, Paul and A. Stewart, *Contemporary Research on Terrorism* (Aberdeen: Aberdeen UP, 1987).

Willrich, Mason (ed.), *Civil Nuclear Power and International Security* (NY: Praeger, 1971), 124pp.

Willrich, Mason (ed.), *International Safeguards and the Nuclear Industry* (Baltimore, MD: John Hopkins UP, 1973), 302pp.

Willrich, Mason (ed.), *Nuclear Theft: Risks and Safeguards* (Cambridge, MA: Ballinger, 1974), 252pp.

Willrich, Mason, 'Nuclear Theft: Risks and Safeguards'. in A.R. Norton and M.H. Greenberg (eds.), *Studies in Nuclear Terrorism* (Boston, MA: G.K. Hall, 1979), pp.59–84.

Wohlstetter, Roberta, 'Terror on a Grand Scale', *Survival* 18/3 (May 1976), pp.98–104.

Notes on Contributors

Paul Wilkinson is Professor of International Relations at the University of St Andrews and Director of the Research Institute for the Study of Conflict and Terrorism, and co-editor of the quarterly *Terrorism and Political Violence*. His publications include *Political Terrorism, Terrorism and the Liberal State,* and *The Lessons of Lockerbie.*

Bruce Hoffman is Director of the Strategy and Doctrine Program of the RAND Corporation's Army Research Division. He is Associate Editor of the quarterly *Studies in Conflict and Terrorism* and author of *Right-Wing Terrorism in West Germany* and many other studies for the RAND series.

Jimmie C. Oxley is a professor in the Department of Chemistry, New Mexico Institute of Mining and Technology, Socorro, New Mexico. She is a consultant for US government agencies.

Andrew Loehmer read Administration Sciences at the University of Constanz, Germany. He has just completed the graduate programme in International Security Studies at the University of St Andrews.

Rodney Wallis is former Director of Security at the International Air Transport Association (IATA) and is widely respected in the international aviation community for his work in co-operation with ICAO and the national aviation authorities of many countries. He is author of *Combating Air Terrorism* (Brassey's [US], 1993).

John D. Baldeschwieler is professor at the California Institute of Technology, Pasadena, California, and was Chairman of the Committee on Commercial Aircraft Security of the National Academy of Sciences of the United States.

David Marshall is Member of Parliament (Labour) for the Glasgow Shettleston Constituency (since 1979) and is former Chairman of the House of Commons Select Committee on Transport.

G. Davidson Smith completed his doctorate at Aberdeen University on a comparative study of British, American and Canadian counter-terrorism policies. This was abridged for publication as a book,

Combating Terrorism. He is a senior analyst with the Solicitor-General's Department in Canada.

Richard Clutterbuck retired from the British Army in 1972 in the rank of Major-General, and became Senior Lecturer, then Reader in Political Conflict at the University of Exeter, 1972–83. His numerous books include *The Media and Political Violence* (1983), *Terrorism and Guerrilla Warfare* (1990) and *Terrorism, Drugs and Crime in Europe After 1992* (1990), and *International Crisis and Conflict* (1993).

Index

152 TECHNOLOGY AND TERRORISM